Volume 5 _____ SAN FRANCISCO BAY AREA

ADAM GOLDBERG
Editor in Chief

DANIELA VELASCO
Creative Director

ELYSSA GOLDBERG
Editorial Director

MAGGIE SPICER
Executive Editor

BONJWING LEE
Copy Editor

-

CONTRIBUTORS
Addison Anthony
Ally Spier
Andréa Morrissette
Austin Langlois
Blair Pfander
Carlisle Williams
Celia Sack
Dan Gentile
Eli Arata
Jessica Battilana
Jim Sullivan
Jonathan Shipley
Kelly Puleio
Leigh Biddlecome
Lou Bustamante
Mallory Farrugia
Marcia Gagliardi
Michael Molesky
Molly DeCoudreaux
Natalie Faye
Nicola Parisi
Sabrina Sucato
Sharon Brenner

WELCOME

Over a third of America's produce and two-thirds of its fruit and nuts are grown in sun-drenched California. The Golden State is also home to the country's largest wine-producing region, the Napa Valley. With unlimited access to great products, it could be said that San Francisco Bay Area (SFBA) chefs have an unfair advantage. But access to great ingredients and fine wine is not enough to stand out. Rising rents and a tighter labor market are making it more difficult to operate a restaurant. And, with the recent influx of capital from successful tech and finance startups, demand for fine dining is increasing, and other types of restaurants are forced to adapt and battle skyrocketing rents or relocate elsewhere.

Because of this new demand, the SFBA has perhaps the most dynamic fine-dining scene in the country right now. It is here that chefs are taking risks, experimenting with novel ways to maximize flavor. Chef Joshua Skenes of Saison prepares an elaborate tasting menu in which nearly every ingredient is dry-aged or touched by flavor-enhancing fire. Chef David Kinch of Manresa casts meat in a supporting role, using it to amplify the flavor of vegetables, the stars of his menu. Chef Brandon Jew of Mr. Jiu's shows how lively and versatile upscale Chinese cooking can be by fusing traditional dishes with local ingredients.

But it's certainly not just the fine dining that makes the SFBA one of the most innovative and diverse dining destinations in the country. Sixty miles south in San Jose we find the largest Vietnamese population outside of Vietnam. Here, the mother-daughter team at Pho Ga Nha serves locally raised chicken in its authentic *phở* and *com ga roti*. Sixty miles north, on the banks of Tomales Bay, visitors spend the afternoon shucking live, sustainable oysters on the picnic tables at Hog Island Oyster Co. And somewhere in-between, in Half Moon Bay, is Dad's Luncheonette. Here, Scott Clark serves a killer grass-fed, local beef burger with a big smile. The abundance of great products, and a concentrated pool of talented cooks affords the SFBA the luxury of obsessing over ingredients and flavor like nowhere else in the country right now.

Ambrosia, Volume 5: San Francisco Bay Area traces the peninsula from San Jose to St. Helena, the Outer Sunset to Oakland, taking a look at the region's food culture, from the origins of the fortune cookie to the impeccably manicured gardens of its leading chefs.

Adam Goldberg
Editor in Chief

Agrelationships

Words and photography by Bonjwing Lee

There's a narrow, five-acre strip of land along the Russian River in Sonoma County that is unusable to its owner, the Seghesio Family Winery. For viticultural reasons, grape vines can't be planted too close to the water. Used as a buffer zone, this land is otherwise perfectly arable. But, instead of letting it sit fallow, the winery leased it out as farmland.

This partnership gives Kyle and Katina Connaughton access to fresh produce just a few minutes away from their restaurant in downtown Healdsburg. Kyle is the chef of Single Thread Restaurant, which opened in 2016 and was awarded two Michelin stars in 2017. And his wife Katina is the head farmer of Single Thread Farm, which has operated on the Seghesio estate since 2014.

She does a lot with the acreage. There's an apiary for honey, and there are about 70 laying hens. From the land, Katina also provides the restaurant with fruit, vegetables, and all of the flowers for the floral arrangements. The farm certainly doesn't provide for all of the restaurant's needs–that was never the Connaughtons' intention. But there's certainly a lot of symbiosis between the two.

Although European restaurants have farmed their own produce, or forged exclusive partnerships with farmers for decades, this concept hadn't caught on in the United States until recently. Some might say that it still hasn't—land and labor costs make it prohibitive for most. And yet, ironically, there's a high concentration of these partnerships in the San Francisco Bay Area, home to some of the most expensive land in the country. Perhaps it's not surprising that they also happen to be among the most highly rated and highly priced restaurants.

Until recently, five of the seven Michelin three-starred restaurants in the SFBA either owned farmland or had an exclusive relationship with a farmer. In 2016, Manresa, the first restaurant of its caliber on the West Coast to adopt such a model, ended its decade-long partnership with Cynthia Sandberg of Love Apple Farm. Of the remaining four restaurants, the two that are in Napa Valley–The

French Laundry and The Restaurant at Meadowood–have farms across the street. The two in the city–Saison and Quince– have farmland north of the city, in Marin County.

In contrast to the manicured rows and stately hoop houses of Thomas Keller's garden at The French Laundry, Fresh Run Farms is wild and rambling. Nestled in the hills above Bolinas, a sleepy surf town about 40 minutes north of San Francisco, the property is owned by the Martinelli family, and currently farmed by Peter Martinelli.

There was still frost on the Brussels sprouts when I arrived with Emilie Winfield early in the morning. Because the farm veins through uneven terrain, the sun arrives late in the day here. And, because of its proximity to the coast, the land is often shrouded in cloud cover. Unlike the perennially sunny Napa Valley, where you'll find strawberries growing in The French Laundry's garden in December, here in Bolinas, the cooler climes require a more seasonal approach to farming.

In 2016, Martinelli and Michael Tusk, chef of the sister restaurants Cotogna and Quince, located next to each other in San Francisco's Jackson Square neighborhood, began working together. Winfield, who had just left Love Apple Farm, learned of the opportunity to work with the pair, and joined Tusks's team as a full-time farmer. Coordinating with Tusk's kitchens, she now works with Martinelli on a daily basis to plan and plant the produce the restaurants need–everything from lettuces and onions to herbs and summer squash, and because of the weather, lots of hardy root vegetables and crucifers.

But there's a lot of land out here. And although Martinelli and Winfield try to plant as diversely as possible, they can't supply all of the restaurants' needs. Like the Connaughtons, Tusk knows this isn't possible. And the yield for what they do grow is high—more than Cotogna and Quince can use. So they started bundling the surplus and making it available to the restaurants' employees at a heavily discounted price, kind of like an internal

Saison Farm

Saison Farm.

CSA program (community—supported agriculture). In 2017, they went one step further by getting a permit to sell these bundles to San Francisco urbanites on the sidewalk outside the restaurants. It was a small program, but it was very popular.

These unintended benefits are what make these farms worthwhile, says Tusk. They may not be the most economically efficient endeavors, but there's altruism at work. And that's an important part of the restaurant culture these chefs want to promote. Christopher Kostow would agree. In 2011, he started a partnership with the St. Helena Montessori School, where both of his daughters are now enrolled.

The sprawling, three-acre farm, which he leases from the school, provides fresh vegetables to both The Restaurant at Meadowood as well as Kostow's more casual, hearth-focused restaurant The Charter Oak. Maximizing the long growing season, full-time garden manager Zac Yoder rotates starter trays and beds to maintain a constant stream of custom-sized vegetables, tailoring the planting schedule to the restaurants' needs.

But, beyond these everyday luxuries, the farm also operates as a classroom for the Montessori students. Here, they get their hands in the soil and learn about sustainable agriculture, helping to plant parts of the garden. There are chickens, llamas, and goats, and stacks of bee boxes at one end–a mini-ecosystem for the kids to explore. And, four times a year, they get a trip up the hill to the kitchen of a three Michelin-starred restaurant to cook community lunches and experience the glorious results of their farm-to-table lessons.

There are others doing this, of course– Dan Barber's pioneering relationship with Blue Hill Farm in New York; chef Blaine Wetzel at The Willow's Inn on Lummi Island, Washington works with Loganita Farm down the street; John and Karen Shields, who just earned their second Michelin star at Smyth in Chicago, are working with The Farm in Bourbonnais, Illinois; and chef Aaron London at AL's Place in San Francisco has been working with Blue Dane Garden since his days cooking in Napa at the now-closed Ubuntu. There are still others yet, seedlings aspiring for growth. The number of chefs and restaurants that are able and willing to make these "agrelationships" work seems to be increasing slowly. The SFBA is undoubtedly leading the charge right now. And that's not surprising, given the demographics of the region—upwardly mobile and environmentally conscious diners who are willing to pay a slight premium for produce with a provenance. Additionally, the exclusive partnerships here are bolstered by the weather; what some describe as the never-ending summer not only ensures the restaurants receive steady stream of fresh fruits and vegetables, but farmers are stabilized by income year-round, not just seasonally. That's a win-win for everyone.

But, of course, there's always a bottom line. And in the restaurant industry, where margins are thin, it's a particularly tight line. Ultimately, these relationships, like a lot of relationships in the industry, hinge on synergy–finding them and fighting for them.

—

The Heart of the Mission Is Made of Corn

Words by Marcia Gagliardi
Photography by Nicola Parisi

It's an unusually hot February afternoon in San Francisco, and Theresa Pasion--"Terry" to her friends--is worried about the *masa*. She imagines her customers driving around, running errands with the *masa*--the dough made from corn that is used to make tortillas, tamales, and more--in their hot cars, and not going directly home with it. Since La Palma doesn't use preservatives, the *masa* can ferment and sour if it isn't stored properly, and she frets that it would reflect badly on her business. "I don't want them to open the bag and think we sold them spoiled *masa*!" When you are known and respected for having the best *masa* in San Francisco, you worry about these things.

La Palma Mexicatessen—its colorful sign with jaunty lettering sprouting off the corner of the butter-yellow building with a bright, kelly-green awning—proudly beams on the corner of 24th Street and Florida. Since it's the last *tortillería* in the neighborhood, you could say La Palma is *hecha a mano* (handmade) in the heart of the Mission.

Many locals know La Palma for its busy counter, serving the kinds of breakfasts that will stay with you late into the day, like *chilaquiles* and *machaca*. Breakfast segues into *huaraches*, *gorditas abiertas*, tacos, and burritos for lunch, and ceviche and *birria* for brunch on the weekends. La Palma's owners feed their customers the way they feed their own families. Older sister and president Ida Ibarra says, "We make beans the way you would at home."

There's a center island crowded with leaning towers of freshly made tortillas—steaming up bags emblazoned with La Palma's trademark palm tree—and refrigerators filled with salsas and guacamole that are made every hour. Customers dance around each other, ordering food, chatting with the cashiers, and surveying the array of tortillas, pantry items, and mountains of *chicharrónes*. There's a hubbub every day, seven days a week, except for Christmas and New Year's Day, when the partners allow themselves to close the Mexicatessen (mindful that many restaurants depend on them for their *masa*).

It's just as busy in the back of the store, where the dry corn is nixtamalized, or soaked in a calcium hydroxide bath to make it easier to grind. After it's cooked, the corn is ground into a snow-like fluff, permeating the air with a rich, sweet scent.

Some of La Palma's *masa* takes a run through the tortilla-making machine, a *molino*, which cranks out tortillas daily for numerous San Francisco Bay Area restaurants, including Loló, Tacolicious, Padrecito, and Tropisueño, plus restaurants in the East Bay. There are even Indian restaurants and Korean taco trucks that use La Palma tortillas. Some *masa* is delivered fresh (and unformed) so that restaurants can press their own tortillas or make other items like *sopes* and *huaraches* in-house. La Palma also makes specialty items like *prensa*, which are large, 10-inch corn tortillas that are grilled.

When you order a taco at La Palma's counter, the *masa* is pressed into made-to-order tortillas—not the usual SF taqueria experience. The restaurant even makes *raspados* (shaved ice drenched in syrup) on the *metate* (stone). The production area is full of ladies in traditional Mexican aprons making *huaraches*, *gorditas*, *tamales*, and *sopes* by hand. One of them is master tortilla-maker, Sara Gomez, who has been at La Palma for 33 years, almost as long as Ida and her partners, who took over the business 35 years ago.

And now, it's the ownership trio of Terry, Ida, and her husband Ruben Ibarra that works nonstop to keep this corn juggernaut chugging. Just like the clangity-clang of the corn running through the grinder (they go through 25,000 pounds of corn a week), they run, run, run. La Palma has nearly 50 employees, and is dedicated to them by keeping the business running successfully. "We know so many people live off these paychecks—a lot of people send money home. They have kids. They depend on us," Ida says. "The thing I am most proud of is that we're still here, and we can keep so many people employed even though we're a neighborhood store."

16

Ida and Ruben Ibarra, two of the three owners of La Palma.

But when they took it over, La Palma was limping along, barely making $50 a day. The previous owners, the Haro family, had suffered a string of tragic misfortunes, and after 30 or so years of running it, in 1983, they sold the business. There was a small counter for *masa*, tortillas, *carnitas*, and groceries, but over the years, the sisters transformed it. The business is said to date back to 1953, but they have a hunch it's even older.

Ida and her original business partners started focusing more on hot food, *masa*, and tamale production. As the number of accounts increased, including catering jobs, the business required all hands on deck. Terry joined the brigade in 1989 when they started building up their accounts and (now-booming) catering business. Ida's husband Ruben even left his well-paying job a few years ago to help out. The three of them are now the partners and owners of La Palma.

Just try interviewing the busy and multi-tasking sisters for an hour. While the three of us were sitting at an outdoor table, enjoying our late afternoon beers in paper cups under the shade of the awning, there were constant interruptions: "Where are the keys?" "Sorry, where should I put this?" The clamor of the old tortilla machine getting wheeled out to make room for the newer, faster one. A rubber-banded wad of cash handed off for the safe. Changes to delivery routes due to street closures. There is no relaxing under the palm tree here. As Terry says, "We're working our buns off!" They do. Their success is built on hard work, and it takes no time to see it.

La Palma's line of *masa* and tortillas is diverse, with *nopal* and chipotle flavors. There are lard-free and sweet *masa* tortillas, too. The tortilleria's organic blue corn tortillas are also very popular. (There is nothing like eating that tortilla, freshly made—its rich fragrance, spongy texture, earthy sweetness, and satisfying elasticity—you want to eat it plain and sweaty, right out of the bag.) Terry says, "It's a wonderful smell, the corn. I wish everyone could just smell it, fresh. There's nothing like it." You can feel her deep adoration for it. They also make a whole-wheat tortilla, and you'd think these corn-obsessed sisters would be ambivalent about it, but they love it. Ida says it doesn't make you feel full, but Terry appreciates its great flavor, color (that isn't too dark), and texture (that isn't grainy).

Although the trio is always innovating, they were using non-GMO corn before it became popular to know the environmental impact of ingredients. They have used the same source for their corn since they took over the business—Adams Grain in Arbuckle, California, which is located northwest of Sacramento. And now, Adams is also the source of their organic blue corn too. Terry proudly says, "People didn't ask, they didn't know. Many are more aware of their food sourcing now. But we have always been non-GMO!"

Terry breaks down the essence of the business: "The handmade tortilla, the corn, and the *carnitas*: that's what built the business. If we stay true to that, you don't even need toppings. All you need is the grease from the *carnitas* and the hot tortilla, and you're in business."

Which they are. The sisters are deeply committed to feeding their community and neighborhood—they haven't raised their *masa* prices in five years. And, unlike most Mexican restaurants, they don't charge extra for their extremely popular spinach tortillas for burritos. Ida sighs, "We see the rents going so high, we don't want the food to go up too. I feel like we owe it to a lot of the low-income families that are being pushed out of the city to keep our prices reasonable."

The sisters note how the Mission has changed. "There are a lot of new people who come into the shop who might not have come to the Mission before, but now they live here," Terry says. "And now they're discovering our tortillas! Our customers are very diverse. It's nice to see."

—

Right: Sara Gomez has been working at La Palma for at least 30 years.

How the Cookie Crumbles

Words by Ally Spier
Photography by Natalie Faye

The fortune cookie: a customary conclusion to any meal at a Chinese-American restaurant worth its weight in *lo mein*. But its origins aren't quite as clear as the wrapper one typically comes in; historically, there's been much debate surrounding the cookie's beginnings. The story behind the sweet send-off, as it turns out, isn't even believed to be rooted in Chinese culture. Despite the fact that the last fortune cookie you ate likely followed something more akin to sweet-and-sour chicken than sashimi, most authorities on the matter have declared the fortune cookie to be a decidedly Japanese dessert.

The "where" and "when" of fortune cookies in the U.S.—California, around the turn of the 20th century—are largely agreed upon. But the precise "who" is a bit more nebulous. One story suggests that Seiichi Kito, a Japanese immigrant who, in 1903, founded Fugetsu-do, the oldest store in the Little Tokyo neighborhood of Los Angeles, was the first to make them. *Omikuji*, cookie-less fortunes written on strips of paper at Japanese shrines and Buddhist temples, may have been the inspiration behind the cookies his bakery sold to Chinese restaurants in both Los Angeles and San Francisco.

Another widely held belief names Japanese immigrant Makoto Hagiwara as the protagonist of the cookie origin story. Hagiwara, a landscape designer who became the official caretaker of Golden Gate Park's Japanese Tea Gardens beginning in 1895, is said to have first served fortune cookies made by San Francisco confectionary Benkyodo to visitors sometime between 1907 and 1914. Hagiwara's cookies are believed to have included their own "fortunes"— thank-you notes tucked inside and addressed to those who helped him secure his job after a racist mayor supposedly tried to fire him.

And a third account suggests that Chinese immigrant David Jung, who immigrated to L.A. and founded the Hong Kong Noodle Company, invented the fortune cookie around 1918. Rumor has it that he recruited a minister to write inspiring scripture passages as the fortunes that Jung would then hand out to local, homeless men in an effort to inspire them to lead more productive lives.

Jennifer 8. Lee, an American journalist and producer born to Taiwanese parents (her middle number "8," self-selected as a teenager, is a symbol of prosperity and good luck in Chinese culture), thoroughly researched Chinese food in Western culture for her 2008 book, *The Fortune Cookie Chronicles*. Her research traced the Jung story back to a friend of the Jung family, who suggested that it was fictional and conjured only to help business; Lee dismissed the Jung option.

Lee's research also led her to Seiichi Kito's grandson, who took Lee to Fugetsu-do's L.A. warehouse. It housed, among other artifacts, a set of black iron molds that she posits may have been used to make the earliest fortune cookies. A subsequent visit to the home of Gary Ono, grandson and historian of the Okamuras, the family that owned the San Francisco Benkyodo store, revealed his possession of similar tools. His black grills, called *kata*, came from an old Benkyodo equipment storage room and were etched with the initials "MH," suggesting they may have been used by Hagiwara himself.

Ono also showed Lee a wood-block printed image that revealed a man in a kimono, holding about a dozen fortune cookie grills that resembled those she'd seen in person. It was marked "1878," suggesting that a Japanese tradition resembling fortune cookie-making had been well-established by that time. Referencing researcher Yasuko Nakamachi's graduate thesis, Lee determined that the Japanese tradition depicted was that of *tsujiura senbei*, savory sesame and miso rice crackers with paper fortunes on the outside, made by family-owned bakeries in Kyoto.

Whether Kito or Hagiwara (or even

someone else quietly baking their own fortune cookies at home), can be credited for bringing a version of the *tsujiura senbei* tradition stateside is still unknown. But concrete evidence points to the idea that the fortune cookie is a distinctly Japanese confection.

So why are fortune cookies served in Chinese restaurants if their roots are Japanese? As with so many things, politics played a role. Before World War II, fortune cookies were known as "fortune tea cakes" and were largely a regional specialty on the West Coast, served in many Japanese-owned, Americanized Chinese restaurants. But more than 100,000 Japanese Americans were interned during World War II, opening up opportunities for Chinese manufacturers. By the end of the war, the fortune cookie had expanded nationally and solidified its association with Chinese culture.

In the decades that have passed since the fortune cookie's full indoctrination into American food culture, production has become less controversial. Modern fortune cookie recipes vary somewhat in their specific ingredients, but are obviously sweeter than the *senbei* that inspired them. Usually, they are a combination of egg whites, sugar, flour, vanilla, salt, butter, almond extract, water, and/or sesame seed oil. Today, their production is largely automated, although they're still made by hand at some places, like San Francisco's Golden Gate Fortune Cookie "Factory," a one-room building for a company that's been in business since 1962. Wonton Food Inc. in Brooklyn, New York is the largest manufacturer in the US, churning out a whopping 4.5 million folded sweet treats daily.

The company's endeavors haven't been entirely hitchless: in the 90s, the empire tried to expand its business to China, but fortune cookies were deemed too American. And in March of 2005, lotto officials briefly investigated Wonton Food Inc. after 110 Powerball players chose the same lucky numbers from the back of a fortune the company had printed. Turns out fortune favors not only the bold, but also those willing to take a chance on a cookie.

—

2
4

The Chocolate Rush

Words by Dan Gentile
Photography by Daniela Velasco

The San Francisco Bay Area is steeped with a rich concentration of artisan chocolate companies bucking industry conventions with a bean-to-bar philosophy, inspired by the characteristic entrepreneurial and innovative traits of the region's inhabitants.

"There's an exploratory, pioneering spirit that's ingrained in San Francisco culture," says Gary Guittard, 71-year old president and CEO of Guittard Chocolate Company, founded in 1868 in San Francisco.

Bean-to-bar starts at the farm. New-school chocolatiers make chocolate with a nod toward tracing the full process. They figuratively have their hands in the soil, sourcing beans with specific flavor profiles and building relationships with farmers to ensure the raw cacao beans are of the highest quality. When roasting the cacao beans in the factory, the chocolate makers treat them like coffee or wine grapes, tailoring the process to the particular beans to bring out the unique flavors that result from growing conditions. Many chocolate companies observe how amino acids interact with sugars to help avoid off-notes, but bean-to-bar innovators take the science further. Santa Cruz-based White Label Chocolate goes so far as to study its chocolate beans at the molecular level.

Bars are typically labeled by cacao content, country of origin, variety of bean, and flavor notes in order to help educate the consumer and maintain transparency of their supply chain. White Label's most popular bar is its "Wild Bolivia," a 72 percent two-ingredient dark bar (just cacao and sugar) that tastes of roasted nuts and orange marmalade.

Although many producers focus on chocolates comprised of beans from a single country (or even specific farm lots), Guittard's artisan line blends varietals, a move that some younger upstarts might consider old-school. It's fitting as it is the oldest, continuously family-owned and -operated chocolate maker in the country. Founded by Gary's great grandfather, Guittard scaled to become one of the largest chocolate wholesalers in the world, supplying companies like Baskin-Robbins. Its location on the West Coast provided a strategic advantage since the trade routes of the time brought lighter and more acidic beans from the Asian Pacific and the Pacific coast of South America. But, as demand grew and new cacao beans flooded the market, overall quality suffered.

"If you look back at the old days, a lot of famous products, like Oreos, used a unique blend of beans that made them really different," says Guittard. "But over the years there was incremental degradation. You change the blend a little bit, but after a series of these changes you don't have the same product anymore."

Guittard still runs a robust wholesale operation, but these days the staff is more excited to talk about Guittard's own bean-to-bar offerings, inspired by another SFBA trailblazer, Scharffen Berger Chocolate Maker. "Before John Scharffenberger, there was no such thing as bean-to-bar; they coined the term," says Megan Guller, author of *Bean to Bar Chocolate: America's Craft Chocolate Revolution (2017)*. In the late '90s, Scharffen Berger founder Robert Steinberg took an internship in France to study Old World techniques like tailoring roast specifications to each batch of beans and learned how to use vintage equipment which he incorporated into his own operation, like a cacao grinder inspired by 19th-century European designs. These methods and tools ran contrary to the practices of industrial chocolate companies and confectioners, who were buying chocolate manufactured to more generic specifications and often using lecithins to mix into their own creations.

Scharffen Berger Chocolate Maker sold to Hershey's in 2005 and no longer practices the same level of artisanship, but served as inspiration for larger chocolate makers like Guittard to explore alternatives to industrial methods. And new producers like Dandelion Chocolate launched (2010) as just two guys playing around with cacao beans in their garage.

"As we were trying to recreate old techniques, we had to build or repurpose

DANDELION
SMALL BATCH
CHOCOLATE

100%
CAMINO VERDE, ECUADOR
2015 HARVEST

We roast, crack, sort, winnow, grind, conch, and temper small batches of beans. Then we mold and wrap each of our bars by hand. By sourcing high-quality cacao and carefully crafting small batches of chocolate, we strive to bring out the individual nuances of each bean.

These beans come from a sustainable farm, and fermentary operated by Vicente Jiminez in Balao...

many of our first tools and machines. That, plus a craftsman mentality, allowed us to start making good chocolate quickly," says Todd Masonis, co-founder of Dandelion. "In addition, we came from the tech world and that Silicon Valley mentality was enormously helpful."

They now have their own cafe and factory in the Mission District of San Francisco where visitors can see the production process up close and sample their full line of bars, including the most popular, a Madagascar chocolate that tastes of strawberry, yogurt, and peach. In addition to bean-to-bar chocolate bars, Dandelion sell confections such as its signature "s'more," house-made hot chocolate (at least 3 varieties), and freshly-roasted cacao beans.

Showing consumers the process helps educate and build demand, but it doesn't address the challenges at origin. One company that's strived to change the way cacao is farmed is TCHO. In 2005, the company formed with two principles: single-origin flavor and affordability. First it developed a flavor wheel similar to those used in wine and coffee. Then it revamped its supply chain.

"TCHO became the first company in the chocolate world to build flavor labs on the farm level to educate farmers on the impact their growing practices ultimately have on the chocolate's flavor profile," says Ari Morimoto, brand marketing director at TCHO. "By enabling farmers to produce their own finished chocolate products, TCHO was able to buy consistently better beans at lower prices while improving farmers' lives." Trusting in the quality gives them the ability to buy larger quantities, which helps everyone win.

Like Scharffen Berger before them, TCHO's innovations haven't gone unnoticed by investors. The tech pedigree of co-founder Timothy Childs, a former NASA engineer, drew initial financial backing from Louis Rossetto and Jane Metcalfe, the couple who started *Wired Magazine*. Although all three have moved on to other projects, the company they built just announced another huge corporate development: acquisition by Ezaki Glico, the Japanese company best known for chocolate Pocky sticks.

Although some might cry sell-out, making chocolate isn't cheap. Investments, like those received by TCHO, allow greater access to beans, more advanced and efficient processing, and wider distribution networks, coincidentally all elements that can lead to that incremental degradation that Gary Guittard bemoaned.

The difference today might just be, well, you. When consumers enter the retail outposts of operations like Guittard, Dandelion, and TCHO, they aren't just wowed by the fancy packaging (which is, admittedly, incredible). They're interested in what's actually in the chocolate, excited to learn about what happens at the farm level, and are armed with palates finely-tuned enough to identify flavors such as dried plum or jasmine.

"People are becoming more and more aware of what's in their chocolate, where it comes from, and the ethics behind it," says Guller. She's seen the trend blossoming on the East Coast as well, where consumers are more skeptical and there's a much higher concentration of confectioners than chocolatiers.

"I don't think bean-to-bar is going to replace Hershey bars and Snickers," says Guller, "but for someone who loves chocolate, it really is a dream to walk into these places."
—

SFBA Bread and Microclimates

Words by Mallory Farrugia
Photography by Daniela Velasco

San Francisco is the American city where food culture is perhaps most rooted in place. As it should be. Surrounded by wine country, swaths of agricultural paradise, and dairy farms where goats, cows, and sheep graze on grassy hills overlooking the Pacific Ocean—this place is extraordinary.

The bread made in the city is a unique representation of place. San Francisco's signature bread is the sourdough. Pioneered by Isidore Boudin in 1849, the original sourdough was (and is still) made with white flour and acidic fermentation from wild yeast and *lactobacillus*, yielding a distinctive tang. Since then, and especially over the last 20 years, the predominant style has evolved in favor of whole-grain flour paired with milder lactic fermentation, resulting in breads with a wider range of flavor and texture. In these breads, you can taste the different grains used, and the subtler qualities that arise from the variations in the baking process, baking environment, and the equipment and setup in the bakery—whether proofing happens in the open air or inside a climate-controlled proofing chamber, for example.

San Francisco offers an ideal climate for sourdough bread-making. Yeast prefers environments in the 78 to 82 degrees Fahrenheit range—perfect for a city that rarely sees days hotter than 85 degrees. And it's dry enough that the dough doesn't get too wet and overactive, but moist enough that finished loaves will stay chewy for days. These conditions have given rise to a golden standard in bread: that Instagram-worthy, open-crumb sourdough levain that has been practically trademarked by the city's iconic Tartine Bakery.

But San Francisco is also a city of microclimates, so a bread that's baked in the Mission could look and taste very different from one baked in the Outer Sunset or NoPa—especially when the bakery environment is relatively *au naturel*, and the dough is allowed to ferment in the open air. Tasting bread from around the city reveals these variations.

3
4

Tartine Manufactory.

Josey Baker of The Mill, a bakery and coffee shop on Divisadero Street in the middle of the city, designed a process to allow his bread to reflect its environment. "What we do here is very much attached to place," Baker says. He sources grain from local farmers and his team mills it in-house. His baking process is designed to bring out the intrinsic flavor of that base ingredient. For Baker, making bread is akin to a conversation between the grains, the earth, the farmer, the baker, the dough, the oven, and the customer. He's honed his process to best serve the grain, making subtle changes to account for variables like shifts in weather. "Bread is a living thing and has a lifespan," he says. "The skill of the baker is deciding when to stop one process and start another."

In neighborhoods nearer to the ocean, bakers are beholden to the shifts in breeze or the sudden onset of fog. Dave Muller, co-founder of Outerlands in the Outer Sunset learned the interconnectedness of place and process by experience. Chad Robertson from Tartine taught him to make bread with simple ingredients and a simple process. At Tartine, the dough is retarded, or cooled overnight, before baking the next day. Muller had no space for retarding or refrigerating the dough, so he left it out overnight. He noticed that, when there was cloud cover, the bakery would get warmer, which caused the dough to become very active. So, he learned to adapt the dough accordingly. The result is a consistently crusty, chewy, levain-style sourdough boule that is unique to Outerlands and its location nearer to the coast. Matt Jones, who now manages the bakery at Outerlands, has figured out a way to refrigerate the dinner boule dough. But the sandwich loaf—of great acclaim among the brunch crowd—still proofs in the open air. "If you wake up in the middle of the night and realize it got too hot, you get in early and bake it early," he explains.

Just north of Golden Gate Park from Outerlands is Marla Bakery, where head baker Sean Ehland is equally attuned to the weather. "When I shut my front door in the morning and there's resistance, I know it's going to be humid," he says.

"That means we'll hold back a touch of water until the mix is complete and then go by feel." At Marla, Ehland bakes with one mixer and one oven—and no climate control. In this minimal, rustic setting he bakes a more svelte sourdough loaf with a tang and hint of extra salinity, which he describes as "mild brackish seawater bread"—a flavor profile and texture that circles back to Boudin's original sourdough, which is thought to have captured the taste of Karl, the nickname of the city's iconic fog.

Each of these breads reflects this place— the region, the neighborhood, the baker and their training, and even the day on which the loaf was baked. Tasting breads made by different bakers in different neighborhoods creates a living map of the city. A bite of bread at Outerlands will remind you of the way the air smelled when you got within earshot of the ocean; a bite of bread at The Mill will signify the city's relationship with the farmlands that surround it. In this way, bread offers a collective taste-memory for the city, even if ephemeral and momentary.

—

Outerlands' head baker Matthew Jay Jones.

THE BAY AREA'S BEST PASTRIES

SILVERADO TRAIL

ST. HELE

SANTA ROSA

NORTH BAY

HEALDSBURG

LARKSF

SAN RAFAEL

FLOURLESS
CHOCOLATE CAKE
{SHED}

PAIN AUX
RAISIN
{M.H. BREAD +
BUTTER}

PEANUT CHOCOLATE
TART
{POSIE}

POINT REYES
NATIONAL
SEASHORE

PACIFIC COAST HIGHWAY

N

STRAWBERRY SHORTCAKE {BAKESALE BETTY}

TARTE TARTIN {FOURNÉE BAKERY}

BERKELEY

SINCLAIR FREEWAY

MONKEY BREAD {MANRESA BREAD}

SAN JOSE

NIMITZ FREEWAY

SOUTH BAY

SAN MATEO BRIDGE

BAYSHORE FREEWAY

DUMBARTON BRIDGE

PANETTONE {FROM ROY}

SAN MATEO

BUTTER CROISSANT {ARSICAULT}

CITRUS TART {CRAFTSMAN + WOLVES}

SAN FRANCISCO

GOLDEN GATE NATIONAL RECREATION AREA

FILLED CRUFFIN {MR. HOLMES}

DOGPATCH

HAM + CHEESE MORNING BUN {NEIGHBOR}

CANELÉ {BOULETTE'S LARDER}

BAKED HAWAIIAN {LIHO LIHO}

BLUEBERRY PIE {THREE BABES}

MISSION DISTRICT

BERNAL HEIGHTS

KOUIGN-AMANN {B. PATISSERIE}

INNER RICHMOND

PASSIONFRUIT MILK CHOCOLATE DONUT {DYNAMO DONUT}

OREOS {BLACK JET BAKERY}

RUSSIAN HONEY CAKE {20TH CENTURY CAFE}

LEMON MERINGUE CAKE {TARTINE BAKERY}

PASTRY LIST BY MAGGIE SPICER   ILLUSTRATION BY KATIE NAPOLI

Every Sunday and Monday in December

Words and photography by Bonjwing Lee

The Silverado Trail moves quickly. Sometimes, too quickly. To the uninitiated, it can be harrowing. The narrow, two-lane road weaves and curves. It's barely lit at night. And turnoffs are poorly marked or hidden. I've driven the trail countless times, and I still miss them.

But every time I swing around that rocky bend where the old Pope Bridge hangs a left towards downtown St. Helena, and the scene widens out onto a silvery row of olive trees, I take my foot off the pedal. I know I'm home. This is Meadowood Napa Valley, where I have spent five of the last six Decembers.

Nestled in the eastern foothills of Napa Valley, this world-class resort has a world-class restaurant. It was here in 2010 at The Restaurant at Meadowood that Christopher Kostow became the youngest American chef to earn three Michelin stars. And it is here that he hosts the Twelve Days of Christmas, an annual culinary event that gathers a glittering cast of chefs from around the globe to his kitchen: twelve nights, twelve dinners. Among chefs, it has become one of the most coveted invitations; among diners, it is one of the most prized reservations. And, as a photographer, I get a front row seat to it all.

My days here are long. I'm in the kitchen early, at 9 am, sometimes earlier. And, after most have turned in for the night, I'm up furiously editing through thousands of photos for morning press.

But Sundays and Mondays, when the restaurant closes, are mine. In the first few years, I used the free time to explore Napa Valley and beyond—sometimes alone, but often with friends in the area. Many of them worked in restaurants and wineries, and had the same days off. Those who weren't catching up on sleep joined me.

We'd stock up on snacks and drinks and drive west into Sonoma County, through undulating hills of velvety green dotted with cows. On a map, it looks like a plate of spaghetti, a tangle of roads weaving through uneven terrain.

Sun out, windows down, the air was thick with menthol as I drove through groves of eucalyptus. They're everywhere here, an invasive species brought from Australia during the Gold Rush. We hit Petaluma and sleepy Sebastopol, and Tomales Bay, where we whiled away the afternoon shucking oysters and drinking wine in the California rays.

At El Molino Central, we had tamales and chicken mole, fish tacos and enchiladas on the picnic tables that line the restaurant's parking lot. It was a surprisingly good find in Boyes Hot Springs, what seems like a footnote of a town just north of Sonoma township. And further up Highway 12 in Glen Ellen is Ari Weiswasser's neighborhood gem, Glen Ellen Star. Open on Sundays and Mondays, when many restaurants are otherwise closed, it became a fixture on our weekend list. From Napa, my friends and I would carpool over the snaking Mount Veeder pass to crowd around bubbling pizzas and brick chickens out of Weiswasser's wood-fire oven.

And, of course, there have been many visits to wineries, from Ted Lemon's biodynamically farmed Littorai, to John Kongsgaard's wild and untamed vineyard on Atlas Peak and the Elysian estate of Continuum, where Chiara Mondavi walked us through her family's manicured rows up on Pritchard Hill.

What a strange experience this is for a boy from the Midwest. Born and raised in Kansas City, Missouri and having spent my college years on the north shore of Chicago and law school years in Ann Arbor, Michigan, winters were always a mix of grey and slush.

Even after five Decembers in northern California, after having settled into a familiar routine here, it still feels unnatural to find juicy, ripe tomatoes at Gott's Roadside, or to polish off a milkshake there, with the warm sun on my back. Not 10 minutes past the Meadowood gatehouse, this burger stand on Highway 128 has become an increasingly frequent meeting place for my friends and me on weekends.

It's not just the climate that seems foreign to me. It's the people too. Napa is a strange mix of tourists and billionaires, hippies and gentlemen farmers.

Around St. Helena, there are all the usual signs of the season. There are Christmas lights and Christmas trees. A giant wreath with a big, red bow hangs on the brick side of the drug store on Adams Street. I find childhood friends catching up over those buttery English muffins at the Model Bakery on Main Street, all of them home from college for the holiday break. And the town's post office crowds with locals dispatching wrapped tidings to far corners of the country. Except everyone's in shorts.

Having grown tired of the day-long excursions of yesteryear, more recently, I've preferred staying close to home base on the weekends. Over the course of dozens of visits to the San Francisco Bay Area wine country—not just the ones in December—I've thoroughly canvassed my dining options. And, as good as many of them are, they're priced for tourists and not exactly convenient. Even the closest meal in Yountville, or the city of Napa at the very bottom of the valley, means a good, half-hour drive or more each way—in the dark, on the Silverado Trail—not to even mention venturing afield to Sonoma like I used to do on weekends, or further, San Francisco.

In mid-2017, Kostow and Nathaniel Dorn, the general manager at The Restaurant at Meadowood, took over the old Tra Vigne space in St. Helena, opening The Charter Oak. I love sitting in the glow of the restaurant's big hearth fire out of which chef Katianna Hong pulls beautifully roasted meats and vegetables, and a killer double-patty cheeseburger. I relished having this closer and better dining option.

From my porch at Meadowood, I hear birds chirp and acorns drop. Otherwise, it's completely quiet here. Sometimes, I'll take my breakfast out there with the newspaper, and wrap myself in a blanket. In the afternoons, the sun can get so hot that I'm forced to retreat inside. At night, I almost always light a fire. It gets chilly once the sun drops below the Mayacamas Mountains on the western side of the valley.

But it's not always like this. The first winter I spent in Napa, it was unseasonably rainy. And, last year, it was unseasonably hot. One year, there were even flurries. But this stretch of California is famously temperamental, a mosaic of microclimates that explains the patchwork of vineyards throughout the region. A matter of meters could mean a sizable difference in rainfall, sun exposure, and wind. Elevation matters a great deal too. The valley floor is much hotter than the mountain ridges that hem the long, skinny Napa gully in on the east and west sides.

Most of these things are a mystery to me, a boy from the flat, prairie plains, where summers are hot and winters are cold; where streets are straightforward, and nobody misses their turn.

But, I'll admit, as the year grows long, I look forward to those late, California days. Of course, there's the excitement and anticipation of the marathon of dinners, the carousel of chefs, and the everyday excitement of working with some of the most dedicated, talented, and passionate people in the restaurant industry. I know that I have a catbird seat at The Twelve Days of Christmas at The Restaurant at Meadowood, and it remains an annual highlight.

But there are those lazy afternoons with the smell of sun and eucalyptus in the air. There's the promise of oysters, if I reach a little, or a juicy BLT just down the road. And, always, there's that silvery row of olive trees that begs me to slow down and stay awhile, every Sunday and Monday in December.

—

The New Napa

Words by Austin Langlois
Photography by Adam Goldberg and
Daniela Velasco

At Napa Valley's newest winery, Ashes & Diamonds, you won't find the Tuscan stone treatments or clay roof tiles that adorn neighboring wineries. The concept is instead inspired—both in wine and design—by California's past, while offering an experience that's distinctly modern. Although the winery's vintages are a departure from the stereotypically-bold California wines, they are also a shift back to the Old World-style of winemaking, one without modern chemical intervention and additives.

And while Ashes & Diamonds may be the splashiest new winery in the valley, it's indicative of a significant trend in California's wine country, one that places greater importance on sustainable farming and light-handed winemaking. Here, it's about the experience as much as it is about the wine. And, it embraces transparency and inclusiveness, rather than the unapproachability and elitism for which much of the industry is known.

This change in winemaking and the approach to the winery experience is evident upon entering the estate where white, minimalistic buildings are configured in a campus-like setup with a communal plaza connecting all of the various vignettes for lounging. Inside, comfortable mid-century modern furniture populates the central area. A black marble bar with accompanying stools expands across the back. It looks more like the living room of Don Draper's bachelor pad than the archetypal Napa tasting room.

Resident chef Emma Sears, who previously worked at Sonoma-based Scribe Winery, offers a local, plant-forward menu, featuring dishes like asparagus with dry-cured olives and tarragon, and house-made tagliatelle with spring pesto, fried Meyer lemon and green garlic, which complement the single vineyard and varietal blends available for tasting.

Ashes & Diamonds also offers guided tours of the property in which visitors can learn about its organic farming methods and sustainability measures—like its use of recycled vineyard water to irrigate the landscaping. It also takes you behind the scenes of the winemaking process. Akin to an open kitchen, the open winery concept shows off everything, from the custom-made equipment to the gleaming wine cellar.

Not only is it a reflection of a more sustainable approach to winemaking, it also tries to satisfy consumers' expectations, something Kashy Khaledi, founder of Ashes & Diamonds, takes seriously.

THE START OF SOMETHING NEW

Ashes & Diamonds is the amalgamation of Kashy Khaledi's Napa winery heritage (his father was the owner of Darioush Winery) and his background in the music business.

Khaledi brought on two terroir-focused Napa winemakers, Steve Matthiasson (five-time James Beard Award nominee) and Dan Petroski (*San Francisco Chronicle's* 2017 "Winemaker of the Year"), both celebrated among oenophiles. Inspired by the collaborative process in the music industry, Khaledi wanted his label to represent a collaboration between these two different winemakers. After Petroski's contract ended, Khaledi brought on Diana Snowden Seysses (of Snowden Vineyards), who is known for her site-specific vintages and "non-invasive," or low-intervention, winemaking.

Generally, Matthiasson leads the winemaking for the vineyards that he farms (both on his own land and the Ashes & Diamonds vineyard on the estate), while Seysses focuses on the single vineyard Cabernets that are sourced from different growers. "They do work fairly collaboratively, despite one person being named as the winemaker for each bottling," said Ashes & Diamonds sales and marketing director Lauren Feldman.

OLD-WORLD WINEMAKING FOR THE NEW WORLD

Both Seysses and Matthiasson are quick to shed the label "natural wine" because they say it has an "unregulated and

undefined" meaning. Instead, they prefer to use terms like "low-intervention" winemaking to describe their return to a classic wine-making process without chemicals and shortcuts.

Splitting her time between California and Burgundy, France, Seysses approaches winemaking with "Burgundian eyes." To her, this means not using fertilizers or herbicides; instead, she naturally cultures the growing ecosystem.

"To have an expression of terroir making site-specific wines, you have to farm organically, if not biodynamically," said Seysses. "It requires an intimate relationship between the winemaker and the grapevine."

Even after harvest, she doesn't rely on chemicals when crafting the wine. "I use natural fermentation parameters, like temperature, pH, and oxygen, to encourage what I want to grow while leaving room for nature to do what it will."

Matthiasson echoes her sentiments; he's been a leader in sustainable agriculture and low-intervention winemaking. "There are a lot of decisions you make in the vineyard, from microbes to cover cropping [a practice of planting crops—like grasses or legumes—to protect and improve the soil], that impact the wine," he said. "A lot goes into not doing very much; don't confuse low-intervention winemaking with laissez-faire."

While it's a winemaking practice that's starting to gain traction with the California wine industry, it's far from new. Littorai co-founder Ted Lemon, who spent 20 years consulting in Napa Valley, acknowledged that slowly the wine culture has begun to shift away from using additives, even though he and others (like Matthiasson and Seysses) have been making low-intervention wines for years.

"Rich, oaky, and bold styles made a lot of people a lot of money," he said. "Now, there is a whole other level of interest in what wineries are doing. People are interested in: 'Who owns this place?' 'What are their values in farming?'"

Laura Brennan Bissell is another winemaker who's also shedding the old, bold-and-overripe Napa style for more lighter-touch winemaking methods. She founded Inconnu Wines, which features affordable, low-intervention wines: The whites are salty and acidic, while the reds are bright and fruity. Last year, she was named a "2017 Winemaker to Watch" by the *San Francisco Chronicle*. "Making wine this way has taught me to be patient," Bissell admitted. "I have to wait until it's ready, instead of forcing it to be."

PURSUING NEW BALANCE
Given the philosophy of Ashes & Diamond's winemakers, it's no surprise that its wines are a sharp departure from the stereotypically-Californian bold flavors and higher alcohol content.

"What's being rediscovered is the sense that California wine made with a lot of restraint can be a great wine," said Matthiasson. "Napa Valley has been written off by people who are looking for more subtlety. It can whisper as well as shout."

This quest for balance has resulted in wines that are moderate in alcohol, which Matthiasson purports are more "harmonious" and better complement food.

David Ramey, of Ramey Wine Cellars, also references this pursuit of balance in contrast to the 20 years of what he refers to as "bombastic" California wines, which have since become pervasive (often biased) stereotypes of California wines, especially Cabernet. California's long, warmer summers can ripen grapes quickly, giving rise to higher sugar content; after fermentation, this results in wine with higher alcohol levels. So, winemakers can control the alcohol content by monitoring ripeness (or sugar content) and adjusting harvest times accordingly. Generally, the riper the grape, the bolder the taste, which is sometimes characterized as "overripe" or "flamboyant."

"Some people, including us, have returned to time-tested, Old World techniques," Ramey said. "[But] the majority of winemakers are

Right: House-made tagliatelle with spring pesto, fried Meyer lemon and green garlic.

Left: Roasted beets with black garlic tarragon vinaigrette and house-made ricotta.

uncomfortable letting nature make the wine. Nature was making wine for 6,000 years before we showed up," he mused.

When asked about the appeal of wine made with this naturalistic approach, he used the analogy of Wonder Bread compared to artisan, hearth-baked bread. "Which would you rather eat?" he asked.

A RENEWED SPIRIT

Behind the Ashes & Diamonds estate, you can't help but notice the char from the October 2017 fires, which burned through 200,000 acres across California wine country.

While the fires destroyed wineries and seared the landscape, the impact to the terroir here will be minimal—if at all. For the soil, it's a natural process. Some of the wine may be affected by the smoke, but winemakers won't know until after fermentation.

The worst tragedy of the wildfires were the thousands of homes destroyed. Carlisle Williams, who works at Ashes & Diamonds, and her husband barely escaped with their dogs and cat at 2 a.m. The last thing they saw was the fire barreling down the street toward their fleeing car.

After sneaking back to their house to survey the damage, she recounted, "Everything except a few cinder block walls was just ash. The fire must have been incredibly hot; our outdoor furniture was just rivers of liquefied silver metal running down our hillside."

Napa has a history of fires and droughts, which makes you wonder why winemakers would submit themselves to such challenging conditions. But, their resilience and perseverance are part of the community terroir, a defining component of what California wine country has been and what it will be.

One of the world's best-known winemakers, Paul Draper of Ridge Vineyards, has seen many changes in Napa Valley during his more than 50 years in the industry. He said he's happy to see a growing group of young winemakers using minimal-intervention methods and relying on the character of the vineyard to meet the increasing demand for more complex California wines.

"Many of our customers are younger and have had more experience [in wine tasting]," he said. "I think they have begun to taste more wines from around the world in a more moderate style. They're also looking at wines to enjoy with food that are refreshing rather than dominating what good chefs are trying to show you."

The interest in this new type of California wine is a movement that's making ripples outside of California wine country. As master sommelier Dustin Wilson (known from his leading role in the documentary, *SOMM*, and his position as wine director of Eleven Madison Park) observes, lighter wines reminiscent of California's 1970s and 1980s vintages are becoming increasingly popular.

"Wines that have more structure and show more of their terroir are what have become cool and in-demand now," said Wilson. "It's refreshing to see actually; wines are so much more interesting now. I love the Ashes & Diamonds project— these types of producers are changing the way Napa is perceived and it's great. The cult wines will always have a place, and they should. The best part about all of this is the diversity available to the consumer."

When asked to speak to this California wine renaissance, perhaps Seysses sums it best when she says, "We live in a very humbling period where we're turning back to the vineyards, to something more holistic. To make something special takes a lot of care. And it's not something that can be explained through analysis; it's something only your heart can tell you." —

Not a Shore

Words by Blair Pfander
Photography by Daniela Velasco

When it comes to top San Francisco Bay Area pastimes, grocery shopping ranks close to day hikes in Muir Woods and ordering burritos at midnight along 24th Street in the Mission. And for good reason. Notable not only for its charm—try to walk past a Bi-Rite Market façade without considering an impulse ranunculus bouquet purchase—but the sheer bounty of fresh produce grown in surrounding farmlands, grocery shopping in San Francisco has become less a chore than an immersive, multi-sensory experience. Add to it a community of store owners, vendors, and co-op members dedicated to educating customers about how, where, and when their food is grown, and you've got one of the most unique grocery cultures in the United States.

Bi-Rite Market

"Excuse me—are you in line?" It's a familiar question to intrepid weekend shoppers at Bi-Rite. Founded in 1940 by brothers Ned and Jack Mogannam and now operated by Ned's sons, brothers Sam and Raph Mogannam, Bi-Rite's two locations (one on Divisadero and the other on 18th Street) are best known for their spectacular selection of fresh, responsibly-sourced produce, unique sundries, superb ice cream, and gourmet deli counter. *And* the crowds. "Right now, it's the Kishu mandarins we can barely keep in stock," says Nick Rubbo, a baseball-capped manager on Divisadero who chats with me on the sidewalk (away from the lines) alongside a bursting display of Cara Cara oranges and local flowers wrapped in craft paper. "We have two bags left, and then that's all we'll see for the season." Scarcity isn't a worry at Bi-Rite, however. The B Corp-certified company educates customers about the unique economics of the grocery supply chain at every level, from growing and sourcing to transportation and farmer wages. "'Community through food' is our motto," says Rubbo. "We try to be transparent at every stage. We even organize field trips down to Half Moon Bay to see where they catch our fish." To that end, every employee is encouraged to step off shift to share stories about product with Bi-Rite customers. A helpful girl with a brunette braid offered me a sample of soft, perfectly-smoked wild Atlantic salmon. Another staff member at checkout whispered an insider tip: "The Dosa Chips," she said conspiratorially. "Seriously addictive. They're at the top of the batch-out receipt every night."

The Ferry Plaza & Farmer's Market

On a recent Saturday at the Ferry Plaza Farmers Market, I was offered this important advice from a man wearing a bandana and gently cradling smoked meat on a baguette: "Come hungry." Whether re-stocking your fridge for the week or looking for a memorable lunch, there's not much you *can't* find at this sprawling farmer's market (open every Tuesday, Thursday, and Saturday). "We're the premiere farmer's market in the

SFBA," said Sean Funcheon of RoliRoti, one of the market's most popular food trucks (before you ask: yes, the porchetta sandwich is worth the 20-minute line). "Everything, and I mean everything, is top-notch." Frequented by tourists and local chefs alike, an estimated 40,000 people shop the market each week for vegetables, herbs, meats, eggs, tofu, oysters and much more. Set against the brilliant, blue backdrop of the San Francisco Bay and Treasure Island beyond, the market hosts a number of certified-organic farmers and ranchers who give educational talks and cooking demonstrations on a weekly basis. Once you've had your fill of the chaos, food aromas, and seagulls—and sampled everything from locally-made cheese to tapenade and granola—head into the Ferry Building to wander the elegantly-curated stalls. Gourmet merchants are a special highlight, including Prather Ranch Meat Company, Dandelion Chocolate, Vive La Tarte, and Hog Island Oyster Co.

Other Avenues

Located at the intersection of Judah and 44th, Other Avenues Food Store Cooperative is exactly the kind of cozy, community grocery hub you'd hope to find in the Outer Sunset's surfer- and artist-populated dunes. "We've been here since '74, so we're a mainstay. It's mostly people who live in a ten-block radius, but we get a few customers from the Outer Richmond, too," says co-op member Steve Watson, who has worked at the shop for four years. "Our buying guideline emphasizes organic and direct-trade, which the community here really appreciates." Every month, 19 co-op members determine the store's policies and product offering, which include a gorgeous selection of produce as well as spices, herbs, vegan-friendly pastries, and apothecary products. The two top sellers week after week? "Bananas and avocados. Always."

The Good Life

The motto at this Bernal Heights and Potrero Hill mini-chain is "Shop where your neighbors shop." It speaks to more than the friendly vibe. Founded in the

1970s, Good Life—which is operated by a board of 70 co-owners—is committed to supporting small farms and local producers over monolith suppliers. Count on a robust supply of California produce as well as locally-sourced cheeses, nuts, and wines. A weekend visit will probably include a short (but worthwhile) wait in line at the deli counter, where perfectly-seasoned rotisserie chickens, comforting soups, and picnic-ready sandwiches are always on offer.

Berkeley Bowl

Oakland and Berkeley natives love a little friendly competition, but one thing they always agree on: Berkeley Bowl is a spectacular place to food shop. Famous for its abundant—and near-overwhelming—produce selection, as well as a unique "bulk" section where shoppers can load up on everything from oolong tea to toothpaste, the Bowl first opened in its 40,000-square foot Oregon Street location in 1977. Since then, it has expanded to a second site at 920 Heinz—which has helped, though not eliminated, the lines, which get intense on weekends. Parking is often a challenge. While everything from fresh onigiri rice balls to burritos are offered and ready to eat on-site, it's the grocery aisles where the Bowl truly shines. Bring a spare tote to stock up on specialty pantry items like bonito flakes, pickled Japanese root vegetables, honeyed peanut butter, and housemade kimchi.

Sigona's Farmers Market

The selection at family-owned Sigona's Farmers Market can be summarized in one word: options. With two locations (Redwood City and Palo Alto), aluminum shelves and wooden barrels teem with an assortment of local fruits, vegetables, dairy, and grains. Are you looking for cremini mushrooms? Here are six varieties. Are dried fruits your preferred Whole 30 snack? Stroll an entire aisle of dried mango, papaya, apple, and peach. Strange and exotic fruits abound, like urchin-esque rambutan and tart mandarinquats, as do artisan cheeses. Over 250 are available. Smoothie-makers and salad enthusiasts will note the extensive bar of supergreens.

Good Eggs

San Francisco is nothing if not a city of app-based conveniences, and for the food-enthusiast, nothing beats Good Eggs. The company delivers "absurdly fresh" groceries to customers' doors from a vast network of local producers and farmers. It's nearly a substitute for shopping at the farmers market, but with the added convenience of picking up toilet paper, teas, and aluminum foil in one stop. Add everything from organic teriyaki bison jerky to herbed goat cheese pretzel knots to your cart—from the comfort of your couch. Busy weeknight chefs would be wise to investigate the meal kits, which range in prep time from 20 to 45 minutes, and include tempting dishes like "One-Pan, Local Trout," "Crispy Chicken Thighs with Blistered Cherry Tomatoes," and "Sheet-Pan Pork Sausage."

SHED

Located in an airy building with a glass façade on North Street, SHED—which bills itself as a "Modern Grange"—is a staple among the well-heeled residents of Sonoma's Healdsburg hamlet, and arguably the most Instagram-able of any grocery in the SFBA. Here, you'll find carefully selected snacks and sundries, everything from beautiful fruit preserves to herbed crackers, freshly baked country bread, and local vintages (it's wine country, after all). It's a great place to assemble a picnic basket, or cool down with a selection of house-made kombucha and kefir water at the fermentation bar. Rounding out the "shed" theme are a selection of high-end gardening tools as well as giftable housewares, like washed-linen napkins and hand-crafted brooms with real corn husk handles because, well, why not?

—

All the Intangibles

Interview by Adam Goldberg
Photography by Adam Goldberg and Daniela Velasco

Joshua Skenes, the chef behind the San Francisco Bay Area's most critically-acclaimed and expensive, tasting menu thinks differently than other chefs in the Bay. He plays on classic tasting menus, but doesn't shy away from inventiveness in his cooking, using rich ingredients in both senses of the word. That is, Saison is unorthodox: Skenes gets city-dwellers who are accustomed to expensive fine-dining to leave behind expectations of red-flesh proteins and caviar served on white plates and starched white tablecloths. Skenes cooks ingredients recently harvested from the running water nearby over a roaring fire, and serves his diners in a glass box near a stream. But, unlike remotely-located, one-off restaurants that merely cook simply and seasonally, Saison delivers premium ingredients with finesse. At Skenes's deft hand, the dishes take on a lightness that might have diners thinking cream and butter are missing from his dishes entirely. He prides himself on making diners feel better when they leave than when they arrived. And, in doing so, Skenes conjures how patrons imagine they might wish to be fed and hosted.

Tell us about Saison, and where you are with the restaurant. Well, hopefully, I'll burn the place down tomorrow and start over again. It was a year after we opened the new space (2013) when I realized that I had fucked up. And I was like, "Fuck, I'm trapped here for a few years now." When we were building the new Saison, my idea was basically the same as it is now. I just didn't have all the details worked out in my mind, and we didn't have the approval of awards and all of that stuff yet.

> "Well, hopefully, I'll burn the place down tomorrow and start over again."

So how many spaces has Saison been in so far? Two.

Did you feel like you had more freedom in the old space? No—mostly because of the physical constraints. There was no fireplace inside. There wasn't proximity between fire and kitchen, workflow, that kind of stuff—it really hinders you. Even now, it's the same thing with Saison; I fucking hate the place. That doesn't mean it's bad; it just means that I've grown out of it. I would love to totally redesign the place; even better than that, it would just be a little place in the woods.

What would you be able to do in the woods that you cannot do at the current location? It's not about the woods; it's about all the intangibles out there, or even the tangible products that you have at your fingertips. You can go outside to a herd of elk in your front yard, then go down to the tidal pools and pull out a sea urchin. Within five minutes [of your place], you open it up, rinse it in seawater, and eat that sea urchin. There's nothing better than that. It can be done differently, but it can't be better—that's really the reference point for what flavor is. When you go to a seafood shack on the ocean, eat oysters and crab, and smell the ocean, it's amazing. There's an intangible factor that really makes the experience better and, at the end of the day, what's food really about? It's about interaction, fun, and celebration. Also, I want to go fly fishing [more often].

Tell me about flavor. Smoke and cooking over fire has been a theme in a lot of your dishes. Could you tell me more about why you use that in your cooking? Fire is just a tool. In America, we struggle with breaking down cooking to its simplest parts— really understanding the *when*, the *how*, and the *whys* behind product and sourcing and what time of year the particular ingredient is [at its] best. What's the best way to catch it? What's the best way to kill it, store it, handle it, prepare it, cook it, and then serve it? It's a lot, right? You can apply that to all products. And then it becomes very complicated just to get the "best" product.

Do you think focusing on getting the best product is something that is unique to Saison? No—I think it's more about focus. I'm pretty sure it's been happening all throughout time. It's just that in America, there aren't the traditions. And there are a lot of traditions that are lost, too, if you look at native traditions. If you look at Old World traditions in France, or Japan. Japan is a great example—if you want to have a conversation about seaweed, well, for 30 generations, you've had that knowledge passed down from person to person, generation to generation. Here's how you store the seaweed. Here's why you lay it on the rocks only for these two hours in the day when the sun's at its brightest. And here's why you bring it back into the wood shack and let it mature for another 12 hours in the day. And so on.

You go down the list and there's all of this knowledge. It's a discovery process for us and it's only been the last few years that I really started to understand that too. It's a really fun process; it's just a really difficult one. I think it takes great energy, effort, and resources. We have our own fishermen, we work with ranchers, and we support these guys with resources. We have two of our own farms, too. It's really expensive to get the perfect product, though there's no such thing as the perfect product, really—it's 10 to 20 times what a normal product costs. Our caviar costs probably quadruple to five times what a good caviar would cost us. So, really, the product quality is the big conversation for

food today. Practices are too. We need a revisioning of how our food practices are handled in America. There are such shitty practices affecting the environment and flavor.

What do you think we can do to increase awareness for product quality in [restaurants]? I don't know. And that's a great question. I don't know if people care, to be honest.

Why do you think that is? There's a lot of effort behind it. You could call up one guy and get all of the shit for your restaurant from him. Most restaurants report from a business standpoint. It's great to make money. But, to me, that's the second most important thing. What I care about is a byproduct of doing something good or creating a good product or a good place.

There is a very Japanese aesthetic to the way that you age meats and use smoke as a flavor enhancer at Saison. Then there was a tasting menu in the old space that had 30-something dishes on it, and there wasn't a drop of butter in any one of those dishes. That's sort of how things were. And it seems like you naturally arrived at many of the same kind of cooking techniques that are used in Japan. At that time, you had never been there. Is there common ground with how you approach a dish and how a dish is approached in Japan? There's a lightness, but depth of flavor, to really good Japanese food that I love. And there's a flavor balance. It's pitch-perfect. When you go to a good Japanese place, you feel satisfied and you feel good. It feels healthy—there's just something about it that feels right to me. What do we want the dish to taste like? What's our end goal in this dish? When we extract flavor from a broth, we don't want it to be salty. We want it to be savory, and have depth of flavor, and represent that particular product in its best form without too many additives. It's just a pinch of sea salt or a drop of Saison sauce [a brew of aspirgillus, seaweeds, and grilled little fish from the SFBA, similar to a smoky, white soy sauce], and that's it. It's like seaweed. You get really great seaweed. It has the right flavor to it. It's

been dried correctly and it's still bright. And its vibrancy is good—then you wind up with a good broth. In comparison, if you put [mediocre] seaweed in it, then you're going to add a bunch of shit to it because it's not the right product to begin with.

You said earlier that it doesn't get better than getting products at their source. Is it equally important to know what to do, or not to do, to products to maximize their potential? No. With caviar, for instance, we spent years working with a guy just to get this particular type of eggs and texture. We trained him on the taste balance we were looking for. "Any eggs are fine. Just make sure it has this particular taste balance and texture," [we'd tell him]. At that point you just need to think about the taste, the flavor, the temperature, the texture, and the mouthfeel. That might mean wrapping a spoonful of the caviar in seaweed, and warming it up, so that the oils start emerging, deepening the flavor a bit. It's those kinds of things. What does this particular product need at this particular time in order for it to taste the most like itself?

It seems like you take a lot of risks at Saison. Is there anything about your approach to cooking, or San Francisco, that facilitates risk-taking? Maybe that's partly me. I'm definitely the risk-taker. But at the same time, it's product-based. So we're pretty much stuck with it. We get a product in for a week that tastes amazing, but then on Thursday, the same product tastes slightly different. So we have to change our cooking depending on the product. That forces us into a situation where we're always changing stuff based around the taste of the product and I think we've gotten used to it. It comes from knowing that we have to change something all the time. That it has got to keep evolving. It's principle cooking rather than recipe cooking, if that makes sense.

We get support from the city. This is the city of the Gold Rush that was founded on people who were willing to take risks, and Silicon Valley—it adds to it.

Saison Reserve Caviar cured and grilled in kelp, spinach cured in seaweed butter and broth.

Do you think that your customers here are more accepting of risk in a menu? I think so. There's no outcry for steak and potatoes. You're pretty much free to do whatever you want. And you can look at some of the other restaurants around; some of them don't even have much to do with cooking, but they're still very successful because there are a lot of people willing to explore.

Well, let me ask the question in a different way. If Saison were located in another city—Chicago, or New York, or Charleston—do you think it would work? Saison as a restaurant? I don't know—probably not. Would another high-end restaurant that was expensive work in another city? I think so, sure. But when we opened the old Saison it was really an exercise in honesty. I started asking myself the question, "Okay, we got this beautiful *poussin*..." It was milk-fed and from this amazing lady, Sylvia Pryzant. You would cook it, and maybe you didn't treat it the right way. So the question is, when you bite into it, is it really the best version of chicken or bird that you've ever eaten? Does this really taste better than other places? If the top 100 chefs in the world came and ate it, what would they say? So we just started asking those questions honestly. And when you assess your own cooking you have got to do the same thing.

Is that a question—"is this the best version of this product?"—you teach everyone in your kitchen to ask regularly? Yes, and it's challenging. Just yesterday I had someone ask me, "Chef, what do you want out of that?" I don't want anything out of it. What does the product need for it to taste good? That's the kind of direction we like to go.

And sometimes it might not need very much, like a sea urchin from the tidal pool. Yes, or anything. It's like those plantains yesterday—we received 50 plantains and here are the best four. You've got an end goal in mind. What's it going to take to make that happen? So you start down this road and there are a million different ways you can go. And it's always a work-in-progress. It's got to be fluid. And then, as long as you are

adjusting and taking those turns properly and using the right methods and paying attention to the product and taste, then you wind up at that end goal.

Do you see any advantage of being close to wine country? Yes. We have proximity to products, a great wine region, and people that come here to make wine. You have sommeliers who want to learn about the winemaking process, who then learn about grapes. It's the same thing with cheese, farming, sea life—all that stuff. It draws people together that wind up creating a good food culture. New York is a restaurant city. Out here, it's more so a food city.

In what way? Well, because, here, everybody wants to eat and everybody loves food. There, you don't have that same access to all of these incredible [ingredients]—although you're starting to now, with the Hudson Valley. [We're seeing] regional food coming back to life. For a long period of time, that didn't exist. And this was one of the few places in the last 30 years that's been like that.

So tell us a little bit about the casual restaurant that you're working on? It's a grown-up, seafood shack with a better wine list and a better playlist.

Are you able to do things there that you can't do at Saison? Yes, because there's a casualness to Angler. It's a casual restaurant that's purely about pleasure: really simple products and really simple cooking.

You can take some radishes and a hunk of butter, and it'll be really great: butter, radishes, and salt—delicious. But I'm not going to serve that at Saison. You want to hopefully provide people with something that's a little more interesting and you want to give them some food for thought sometimes, too. It's like the beet dish—you've heard of the beet dish before, right?

Tell me about it. We poach the beet in its own juice until it's tender. Then we hang it above the fire and turn it slowly, to concentrate its flavors—it turns into a super beet, a very beet-y beet, the most beet-y beet you've ever had. It's like beet meat. Then we roast it like a piece of meat, basting it with butter and aromatics while it's on the grill. And we sauce it with beet sauce and some freshly harvested bone marrow. It's a simple dish. But it takes a really long time to make because a lot of work goes into it. You don't necessarily always have the luxury of spending so much time and effort on a dish in a really casual restaurant.

So what do you cook at home? I like an elk chop and some collard greens. That's about it. In fact, my wife just made me some deer that we got in Hawaii and some rice with hot sauce and broccoli. Pretty straightforward and super simple. I always eat super simply at home.

So the seafood shack is different from the place you're building in the woods? No. The one in the woods is called Skenes's Ranch, and it's being built. The seafood place is called Angler, it'll be here [S.F.] and [also] in L.A. You'll be able to come in for a simple salad. Or you could get a grilled whole fish, order a bottle of DRC [Domaine de la Romanée-Conti], and five pounds of caviar, if you want. It's that kind of place, where everything is completely à la carte; there is complete democracy in decision-making in terms of what you want your dish to be. There are no composed dishes. I love to go to eat where you just get one product on a particular plate, and it's hyper-focused, it's really delicious, and then you can assemble the menu however you want. Because, in a place like that, everybody feels differently every day. Sometimes you want some wild boar. Sometimes you just want a slice of fish. And so, in this particular place, you can pretty much get anything you want.

What can you tell us about Skenes's Ranch? It's a place in the woods where I can serve that piece of elk and that sea urchin from the tidal pool. You're in an area where you have all of the resources around you; the mountains, the ocean, the forest, the pastures, and the rivers are all within 30 minutes of each other. It's ultra-diverse in the range of natural resources and so it provides limitless options of what you can make. It's not just the

immediate cooking, but also the [fresh] products you can have for your own pantry. I go out to the deep ocean and harvest a bunch of sea water and bring it back to my little glass smoke shack, where I put the salt in and light a little fire in the middle. It reduces down and you have this incredible barbecue salt a week later. That taste is locked in. The air is pure. I can hang an elk outside to dry-age in the cool, forest air. I can get a salmon and I can [treat it with] the *ikejime* method [slaughtering fish in a way that maintains the quality of its meat] and I can string it up and put it in the river and let it bleed itself in the river, so it has that purity of mountain water. And I can get the water out of the river and drink the water, which has this amazing taste to it. I can go in the front yard and pick an herb 60 seconds before it's eaten. That's when flavor really changes. It's just about flavor.

—

First of the Season Peas.
Flash poached peas in a pea and seaweed broth then double shucked. Broth made from the grilled pea shells and sorrels. Topped with pea skins dried above the fire.

Omakase Rising

Words by Jonathan Shipley
Photography by Daniela Velasco

Omakase, which translates as "I leave it up to you," is a fixed-price, set-menu Japanese dining experience—and it is proliferating throughout the San Francisco Bay Area. The chef decides what the customer will eat, not the other way around. Michael Bauer, a writer for the *San Francisco Chronicle*, notes that the area's *omakase* trend started in 2014 when Kusakabe opened. Kusakabe currently offers omakase menus that start at $98. The dishes are prepared *kaiseki*-style. Based on the essential tenet, "*goshoku, gomi, gokan, gohou*" ("five colors, five tastes, five senses, five methods"), *kaiseki* is a traditional, multi-course Japanese menu composed of small dishes that focus on being present in the moment, including the season. Since the opening of Kusakabe, to much success, many other restaurants in the city, ranging from Omakase to jū-ni to Ijji, Wako, Sasaki and Kinjo, began offering multi-course *omakase* meals.

San Francisco's first Japanese immigrants arrived to the area in 1869, and though there was a mass exodus during WWII because of Executive Order 9066 that sent people of Japanese ancestry to internment camps, San Francisco has the fourth largest community of Japanese descendants in the nation. With that, and with an increase in affluent diners, sparked in part by an increase in tech jobs within the SFBA, Japanese cuisine is now a staple in the city. Some menus are as inexpensive as $100 for a night of high-caliber Japanese cuisine. Others can run upwards of $500 per diner. Aside from the demographic factors, San Francisco restaurant critic Jonathan Kauffman surmises that the rise of *omakase* meals has something to do with "the maturation of Americans' understanding of sushi and the acceptance of tasting menu formats." Sushi is no longer an exotic meal to indulge in from time to time. Now, sushi is readily available in supermarkets and airports. He also speculates that low labor costs—having a single- or two-chef restaurant, for example—offsets high ingredient prices.

This boom in Japanese restaurants has tried to keep apace of the increasingly sophisticated diner. Now, San Franciscans have access to *makizushi*, *nigirizushi*, *oshizushi*, and much more made by some of the city's best chefs.

To become a master sushi chef, an *itamae* in Japanese, meaning "in front of the board," takes up to 10 years of training (and sometimes more), from rice cleaner to apprentice to chef. Masaki Sasaki, for example, has over 30 years of experience as a sushi chef. He has earned a Michelin star for his eponymous, 12-seat counter *sushiya*. For $180, guests are served four courses that include 14 pieces of *nigiri*. The restaurant is one of the most traditional sushi experiences in San Francisco, serving horse mackerel, sea eel, and house-cured sardines in a calm, pristine food-first environment. All of the fish are flown in directly from Japanese waters except for the albacore tuna.

Ijji, near Buena Vista Park, seats only 15. It's an intimate meal of 19 courses, running $155 per person. One can enjoy pike eel with plum paste in bonito broth, massaged octopus, and barracuda with shiso leaves. Chefs Billy Kong and Kua Catuang offer bold interpretations of *nigiri* while still allowing for the fish to shine through. The chefs prepare customary ingredients, like *koshihikari* rice and *akazu* vinegar, while using traditional preparation techniques to create their own unique dishes, like *tamago atsuyaki*, for instance, which includes blue shrimp.

Meanwhile, at jū-ni, chef Geoffrey Lee, one of *San Francisco Chronicle's* 2016 Rising Star Chefs, offers his own striking takes on sushi. Working at Akiko before starting his own restaurant on Fulton Street in the NoPa (North of the Panhandle) neighborhood, he served horsehair crab, trout roe, and seared *nigiri* topped with black caviar. This Michelin-starred restaurant is intimate, seating only 12.

Places like Ijji and jū-ni highlight the fact that, though sushi and sushi-making are a time-honored tradition, it is not set in stone. Kong, Catuang, and Lee are proving this by putting one's own personality into even the simplest of dishes. Rice can be more than just rice. A piece of fish can be more than

Left: Kake udon, hand-rolled udon with two fishes broth and scallion, Rintaro.

Next page, left: Hanetsuki Gyoza. Becker Lane Berkshire pork gyoza with chicken foot jelly and "wing", Rintaro
Right: Kinki No Nitsuke. Whole Monterey rock cod simmered in sake, shoyu and ginger with komatsuna greens and courtyard sansho leaves, Rintaro.

simply protein. A small change in the combinations of flavors can create a new dish, and a new experience, entirely.

The *omakase*-style dining experience is a trend that continues to rise in the SFBA. It is particularly popular amongst the SFBA's tech crowd, wealthy folks with discriminating tastes, and those who want a celebratory night out by visiting the restaurants of celebrated chefs. The price for a meal can be daunting.

Hashiri, arguably the highest-end Asian restaurant in all of the city, offers fixed menus that span upwards of $500 per diner. It pairs its menu with rare sakes and wines. Hashiri pays attention to the aesthetics of the dining experience, with walls bedecked with pieces by the city's trendiest artists. The sushi counter is made of Japanese cypress. The ceiling is illuminated with scenes of the changing seasons. Under chefs Tokunori Mekaru and Shinichi Aoki, the restaurant replicates a high-end Tokyo dining experience in San Francisco (there is a sister restaurant in Tokyo, as well). The expensive menu includes a journey through a traditional *kaiseki* meal and *edomae* sushi progression with a private chef, using hyper-seasonal ingredients and fish, such as big-eye snapper, fluke, saba, toro, and uni, directly from Tsukiji fish market in Tokyo. It's these higher-end establishments, like Hashiri, where moneyed diners are welcomed into an inner world—spartan yet adventurous, traditional yet trendy, experiential and delicious, worldly and yet just around the corner.

With clear-eyed goals to create the best meal possible using the freshest ingredients, chefs are demanding more from San Francisco's diners. By eliminating choices from their menus, chefs ask diners to put their evening into the chefs' hands. Knife at the ready, these chefs are cutting through not only mackerel and squid, tuna and marlin, but through ways of giving diners experiences for guests on their own terms.

—

Hodo Soy is Disrupting Tofu in America

Words by Jonathan Shipley
Photography by Eli Arata

Once upon a time there was a prince. His name was Liu An. He lived 2,000 years ago in China, during the Han Dynasty. According to legend, the prince desired to help his ailing mother, who wanted to eat soybeans but could no longer chew them. So, he crushed the beans into milk, from which he made a curd. And thus, An created tofu.

Once upon a time there was an author. Her name was Frances Moore Lappé. Some 2,000 years after the prince created tofu, she published a book. In 1971, *Diet for a Small Planet* was the first major book to discuss the environmental impact of meat production. She introduced—to Western audiences—a curd high in protein made from soybeans. And thus, Americans were introduced to tofu.

Once upon a time there was an investment banker. His name was Minh Tsai. He immigrated to the San Francisco Bay Area from Hong Kong wanting to start a food business. Recalling his childhood visits to tofu shacks in Vietnam with his grandfather, he wondered why he couldn't find that flavorful tofu here in the United States. He decided to try to make his own. He started selling it at local farmers markets, and the business grew. Thus, in 2004, Hodo Soy was born.

Today, Hodo Soy is regarded as one of the best tofu producers in America. Tsai works with both local and international star chefs to change people's perspectives on tofu. He also distributes Hodo Soy products across the nation, from Whole Foods Market to 99 Ranch, aiming to connect with a range of consumers. He is even the tofu supplier for Chipotle. No mere prince, Tsai has become king to a vast, tofu empire.

"Tofu was introduced as a vegetarian food that would save our environment. Then, it was pitched as a food that would save our health," Tsai says. "Even though these claims are valid, the lack of flavor and taste did not help its popularity." Hodo Soy has now been around for 15 years, and in those years, Tsai has continued to educate consumers about how delicious tofu can truly be. He's had his work cut out for him.

If you think tofu is bland and chalky, you haven't had good tofu. "Good tofu has wonderful flavor and texture," he says. "Tofu has tasting notes: nutty, buttery, beany. Our tofu is made from our rich and creamy soy milk—high in protein and fat—and the taste and nutritional content reflect this." "Tofu," he says, "doesn't just have utilitarian virtues." "You don't eat tofu only because it's vegetarian, healthy, or because it will avert a dystopian future. You can eat tofu because it is delicious."

The present is bright at Hodo Soy, and the future, it seems, brighter still. Hodo (meaning "good bean" in Chinese) is located in West Oakland. Its beanery is an airy, 12,000-square-foot production facility that is environmentally efficient. Traditionally, making tofu requires a lot of electricity and water. Hodo invested in a steam boiler to power its milk-making unit. "We use large, 1,000 gallon cooling tanks to chill tofu. The water is sanitized and recycled, saving more than 15,000 gallons of water weekly. The hull and pulp of soybeans are also used as organic feed for ranchers in Sonoma, and a small portion is being tested as flour for baking," says Tsai. From this facility, a wide gamut of soy-based products emerges. Hodo produces tofu puffs and five-spice tofu nuggets. It produces Sichuan mapo tofu, tofu veggie burgers, and an impressively diverse selection of *yuba*, or "tofu skins." In fact, Hodo Soy is the only producer of fresh, organic *yuba* in the country, and it's a pretty special ingredient. According to Tsai, "Making *yuba* is a dying art. There's only one way to make it, and you can't hurry it up—it's like making cream become creamy."

It's been a while since Tsai was a child, walking with his grandfather on weekends to the food stalls of Vietnam in search of the best tofu. Luckily, one doesn't have to go to Vietnam to find the best tofu. Nor does one have to go back in time to the Chinese kingdom of princes to find tofu good enough for royalty. All one has to do is find Tsai's Hodo Soy label on the package.

—

Founder & CEO of Hodo Soy, Minh Tsai.

Top left: After the soy milk is coagulated, a cloth is used to press soy curds into the desired shape.
Top right: Harvesting yuba. Yuba is the thin veil that forms on the surface of rich and creamy soymilk. Bottom: The yuba sheets are hung to cool.

Prior to cutting the yuba into noodles, the sheets are seared to bring out the yuba's natural flavors.

Deli Diaspora
Jewish Delicatessens Schlep to California

Words by Addison Anthony
Photography by Daniela Velasco

"Delicatessen" comes from the Latin adjective "delicatus," meaning "luxurious." In central Europe, from where most Ashkenazi Jews emigrated to the United States in the late-19th and early-20th centuries, foods such as cured meats and sweet pastries were valued highly, and were only purchased for the most special of occasions at the delicatessen. The deli, which would later soar in popularity as a community gathering spot and cornerstone of Jewish-American culture, began as a gourmet food shop. Pastrami meat, kosher pickles, *matzo* ball soup, *challah*, chocolate *babka*, potato salad, bagels, lox, *blintzes*, and *latkes* once belonged exclusively to the then-rare and obscure canon of Jewish cuisine.

Today, delis are less popular than they once were. In the 1930s, more than 1,500 Jewish delis operated in New York City alone. Now, fewer than 200 delis remain in operation across the country—and many are in the country's fourth largest Jewish community: San Francisco, California.

In 1848, a massive influx of Ashkenazi Jews fleeing persecution and chasing the promises of the Gold Rush arrived in the newly-developing settlement of San Francisco. Because the community was just getting on its feet, Jews were able to take a leading role in shaping foundational institutions and infrastructure, as opposed to attempting to carve out a niche in an already-established social hierarchy as they had done in New York and most of the Northeastern U.S. The success of these pioneering immigrants led to a sharp uptick in the social status of the Jewish community in San Francisco. This newly-obtained affluence led San Francisco's Jews to become early adopters of Reform Judaism, meaning that West Coast Jews were more willing to bend their cultural norms to American social norms than their East Coast counterparts.

Deli culture, as we know it, was popularized by the first generation of Jewish immigrants living in New York. In the late 19th century, delis began serving traditional prepared foods for the exploding Jewish communities of

Manhattan and Brooklyn. They provided a sense of nostalgia for first- and second-generation immigrants. *Challah, knishes,* and *bialys* began appearing on New York streets. Katz's, one of New York City's most famous spots known for its brusque service and exemplary meats, opened on the Lower East Side in 1888. Delis hit their stride in N.Y.C. in the 1920s. Signature sandwiches like the Reuben became standard fare in the city.

By the mid-20th century, delis had become associated with the rising status of Jews in America. Delis represented integration. And deli food, like the pastrami sandwich, which was featured in an ad with Coca-Cola in the 1970s, became mainstream, American staples. Deli food came to symbolize secular Judaism—something American Jews could *kvell* about (that is, be proud of) without fear of retribution.

Today, the Jewish population in the San Francisco Bay Area hovers around 400,000. The deli culture that has sprouted in San Francisco is distinct from the famous haunts of New York City and Los Angeles. As immigrants once adapted the Jewish deli to their culture on the East Coast, so too, the deli has had to mold itself to the culture of San Francisco.

Two San Francisco delis illustrate this distinctly Californian departure from the old-school standards. They don't focus so much on kosher or tradition, but instead blend in health-oriented ingredients and terminology that has become the center of Californian cuisine, like organic avocados and antibiotic-free meat products. Both of these establishments have branded themselves as a sort of deli-with-a-twist.

Wise Sons in the Mission District of San Francisco was founded in 2011 by two descendants of Jewish deli owners in Boston, Evan and Ari Bloom, after the brothers successfully hunted down a family pastrami recipe and began cooking the beef in their own backyard. "We couldn't find the experience and the food that we grew up with, so we started to make it ourselves," says Evan Bloom. The pastrami sandwich is a building

Smoked salmon bagel, Wise Sons.

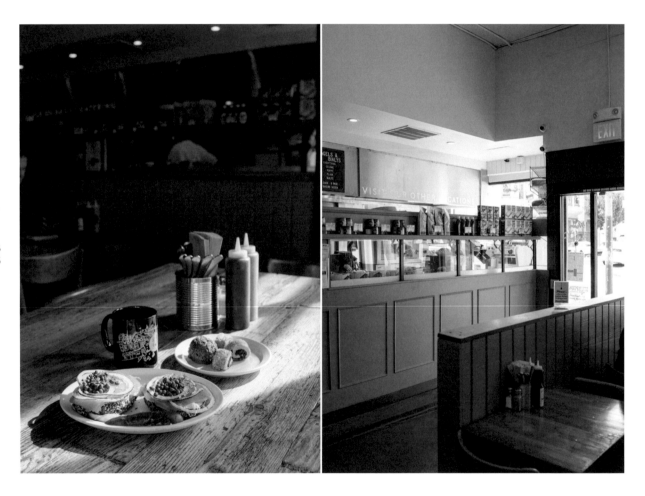

Open-faced smoked salmon bagel and rugelach, Wise Sons.

block of deli cuisine: layers of sweet, tender, and fatty meat piled high atop rye bread and dressed with a glob of spicy brown mustard.

The walls are adorned with overlapping family photos, while newspaper clippings are plastered on an overhanging kitchen fixture. Using fresh, California ingredients, it offers a contemporary, West Coast take on classic, Jewish deli recipes.

Because San Francisco Jews were not living in relative isolation as they were in New York, and the Jewish community was integrated more quickly and thoroughly in the SFBA than on the East Coast, the identity of the Jewish deli on the West Coast became fractured. "When you talk about deli culture, you're talking about restaurants that are 50, 60, and 70 years old. Even in L.A. those restaurants are from the 1930s and 1940s. San Francisco just doesn't have restaurants from that time. And we're a smaller city! We're not New York or L.A., that's constantly turning 24 hours a day and can have these massive menus. The old-school Jewish deli has a menu the size of a phone book, and that doesn't really fit the culinary pantheon here."

Secularization of Jewish communities in S.F. has also impacted the deli experiences. "I think there is now a strong Jewish community, but they don't go to synagogue, they don't keep kosher. They get their Jewish experience by going and having a bagel or a pastrami sandwich. You'd be surprised how many Jews come to Wise Sons on Yom Kippur when they're supposed to be fasting because they're like 'I'm Jewish. I'm supposed to be doing something but I just don't know what it is!'" Bloom says.

Bloom describes the different approaches taken to appeal to a younger, California generation. "We use beef that's never had hormones or antibiotics; none of the classic delis do that, none of them. We offer vegetarian options, we have a few playful items that speak to who we are." But despite some alterations, Bloom says the restaurant serves the same purpose that delis have always done. "A deli is a neighborhood restaurant, and they're all a

personification of their owners. When we opened, Wise Sons was us. And it still is."

Chef-owner Adam Mesnick of Deli Board in the SoMa (South of Market) neighborhood openly disputes his restaurant's definition as a deli, because he doesn't think it's a sustainable definition in S.F. after watching several establishments open and close quickly in the early years of the new millennium. "We do things a little differently…I think we do a good job of creating a new type of deli atmosphere that people are excited to try."

Mesnick attributes the lack of delis to the lack of availability. "There [are fewer] people making Jewish deli food on a wholesale level here, so you fall into a where-do-I-find-this kind of trap," he says. "Sandwich bread here has been a challenge and rye bread especially, so we've kind of moved away from your typical Jewish deli, but the intention of opening was also to remove some of the aesthetic that people don't love about delis, the cases of meat and everything. I don't know that the younger folks really have an appetite for that."

Mesnick can also trace his deli dreams eastward; he grew up around a Jewish family restaurant in Cleveland. Deli Board markets itself as having Midwest roots, East Coast flavors, and a Left Coast twist. Although the restaurant doesn't define itself as a traditional, Jewish establishment, its menu features deli mainstays like corned beef, pastrami, egg salad, and more. The restaurant is rooted in the Jewish deli, but it's not something that it uses as a marketing tool.

Although the California eateries have taken liberties with the deli definition, that is also part of the tradition. Deli owners on both the East and West Coasts added turkey to their menus in the 1950s to appeal to American consumers, and they succeeded; turkey is now a mainstay on deli menus from Katz's in N.Y.C. to Miller's in San Francisco.

Having associated themselves as a purveyor to wealthier Jews in pre-war

New York City, Jewish delis have been adapting to the American market for over a century. But where is the future of deli culture heading? "I think everywhere is having challenges with the deli. I think a lot of them in the big cities have been unable to raise the prices as quickly as they needed to keep up with, say, brisket prices skyrocketing over the last couple of years," says Mesnick. Although delis may be having a hard time across the country, the roots to hold them in place run much deeper in places like New York and L.A. But one wonders whether West Coast counterparts have mutated beyond recognition as delis, or whether their adaptations will take root.

As S.F. tries to define its version of the Jewish deli, East Coasters remain skeptical to the cause. Upon hearing the announcement of another new S.F. deli venture, Rachel Levin of *The New York Times* wrote, "A real Jewish deli in San Francisco has always been as tough to come by as a California-style burrito in Manhattan." Deli owners in San Francisco don't believe they are the same as their East Coast counterparts. Instead, they prefer to highlight the fact that they enjoy the lack of tradition. Maybe that's just how they like it in the City by the Bay. —

Finding Phở in Little Saigon

Words by Sabrina Sucato
Photography by Adam Goldberg

Little Saigon is *not* Chinatown.

Unlike the mini metropolises of New York City and San Francisco, Little Saigon lives just off the radar of tourist itineraries. Although it operates near the heart of bustling San Jose, it sits far enough away from the city center that most people stop at neighboring Japantown instead of driving the extra few blocks to Story Road, the microcosm's unofficial entrance.

If only they knew. Silicon Valley's Vietnamese mecca may not seem like much on the outside, thanks to strip plaza facades and understated signage, but it harbors culinary wisdom that spans generations and attracts the largest Vietnamese population outside of Vietnam.

Let's get the obvious out of the way. As one might expect, there's a lot of *phở*, or Vietnamese soup, in San Jose. Like pizza for Italy and tacos for Mexico, *phở* has risen in fame to become Vietnam's signature dish in the United States. As such, *phở* is as common as water along the coastline of California. Good *phở*, on the other hand, is like gold on a treasure hunt—difficult to discover, but always worth the effort.

"The only [Vietnamese] food that [Americans] recognize is *phở*," observed De Nguyen. Nguyen capitalized on this fact three years ago when he and his business partner Jacinda Do opened Pho Tick Tock. Here, appearances can be deceiving. Inside this unassuming restaurant, situated in a strip mall just outside of Little Saigon, Old World flavor meets modern innovation.

Phở is front and center on the menu. It is the restaurant's pride and joy, embodying the ideals of traditional Vietnamese culture. "Beef *phở* is best," Nguyen declared, adding that chicken is the more contemporary variation. To develop the signature *phở*, he and Do invited local residents to taste-test recipe variations for the first three months of the business. The result is a *phở bò* that is as aesthetically pleasing as it is umami. The *phở* is served "deconstructed," with a bowlful of broth accompanied by a plate laden with multiple styles of beef, including tendon, brisket, tripe, and meatballs.

Tick Tock's *phở* is hot, and not just because it is on-trend.

"When you eat *phở*, you need to eat it hot. You want to sit down and enjoy the *phở* for an hour," Nguyen said. Embracing the idea of *phở* as a communal dish, best enjoyed over conversation with family and friends, Pho Tick Tock serves its soupy concoction in custom bowls that retain heat for hours. Even as the minutes tick (tock) on the clock, the broth stays warm.

If Pho Tick Tock is the modernization of Vietnamese cuisine, Pho Ga Nha is a return to cultural origins. Owned by mother-daughter duo Thuy Hoang and Ivy Tran, the Little Saigon eatery focuses on chicken, the ingredient of the commoners. It embraces chicken as the everyman's (or everywoman's) fare and spotlights it throughout the menu. The chicken, which relies on powerful spices like ginger and anise, requires half a day of cooking to ensure it melts in your mouth.

"Everything we make is by hand. We don't make [anything] until it's ordered. We don't have noodles on the side and chicken chopped up," said Tran. Her mother, Thuy Hoang, runs the kitchen, aided by her unofficial culinary education during her childhood in Hue, Vietnam. As the second eldest, she took on the role of cooking for her parents and her seven brothers and sisters at an early age.

"She's always had a responsibility for food and people," Tran enthused. That responsibility translates to simple, flavorful dishes like diner favorite *cơm gà rôti*, a rotisserie chicken with tomato-infused rice, and sugarcane juice, a sweet nectar made from pressed sugarcane. The food may be "no frills," but that is what makes it so attractive.

Like Pho Ga Nha, Banh Cuon Tay Ho embodies the rewards that commitment and cultural integrity can bring. David Pham opened a second location of Tay Ho in San Jose after he declined a job relocation to Nashville in December of 2000. To escape unemployment, he partnered with his cousin, Mai Nguyen, the founder of Tay Ho Food Company, to expand the family operation. Pham oversees Banh Cuon Tay Ho and its sister spot in Sacramento, while Nguyen runs the food company, which manufactures Vietnamese specialty products for a global market.

Pham credits *bánh cuốn*, thin, flour dough sheets filled with meat and vegetables, as part of the secret to the restaurant's longevity. If the dish's popularity is any indication, it may soon rival *phở* as the most recognizable Vietnamese food in the U.S.

"We make flour sheets fresh every day by using a special steamer, which is an old-fashioned way. We don't use the new method—pan-fried flour sheets," he said. Tay Ho's *bánh cuốn đặc biệt*—known to regulars as #11 on the menu—is the long-standing favorite for good reason. Not only is it a steal for less than $10 per order, but it's offered with traditional Vietnamese options, like ground pork, mushrooms, and *nước chấm*, a fish sauce made in-house with fresh lemon juice.

In such a restaurant-saturated area as Little Saigon, Tay Ho and its counterparts distinguish themselves with an attention to detail and a commitment to the history that defines the cuisine. Are they holes in the wall? No doubt. Yet through those holes seep decades of experience and tradition that whisper to outsiders and draw them in through word-of-mouth. Their siren call is spreading, and Silicon Valley may not be able to contain it much longer.

—

Right: Phở Regular. Flank, fat brisket, and tendon, Pho Tick Tock.

Finding Your Compass

Interview by Michael Molesky
Photography by Adam Goldberg and
Daniela Velasco

In 2003, you would have met Pim Techamuanvivit, the Silicon Valley researcher. In 2009, she would be Pim, the author of pioneering food blog *Chez Pim* and publisher of *The Foodie Handbook*; in 2012, she became Pim, the jam maker and Good Food Award winner; in 2014, she is, as we know her now, Pim, the freshly minted restaurateur behind San Francisco's Kin Khao—a boisterous Michelin-starred establishment in an incongruous Union Square location that redefined people's expectations of what Thai food should be. Bangkok-born and globally bred, Pim seems to thrive wearing different hats, and certainly doesn't intend to stand still. In conversation with *Ambrosia*, she opens up about her unorthodox path to the restaurant world, the roots of her passion for food, and a peek at some exciting chapters ahead.

What was your background before you dove into food professionally? I came up to the San Francisco Bay Area after studying cognitive science in graduate school and worked in Silicon Valley for many years.

When I finished my PhD at UC San Diego, I took a summer research gig in Silicon Valley that led to a full-time job. In academia, you come up with a research concept, write your grant proposal, and then six months later *maybe* hear back about whether you get funded. Six months after that, you get to put your idea into some form of work. I had a lot of fun studying geeks [in Silicon Valley] and trying to understand how people work, until one day, I realized, "Oh, wait, I don't really want to manage a big research group; maybe this isn't what I want to do." That was when I started writing a blog, a couple of years before I left Silicon Valley. Because my research was largely based in Europe and I was already dining out a lot, I started writing about food. It made for a good story in the early years of the blogging craze—this Asian girl, traveling, and writing about French food. It became a thing.

My epiphany was that I don't want to wake up one day at 75 years old, and realize that I haven't really done anything I wanted to do. If I don't do it now, then when?

It sounds like those European dining expeditions really helped one career dovetail into another? I've always loved food. I was raised in Bangkok with very good food around the house. My grandmother was an amazing cook. She made everything from scratch, so I was used to really great food. I've also always been picky about food, but not in the sense of dietary restrictions. If it doesn't taste good to me, I don't eat it. I don't care who cooked it.

I may also be part of one of the last generation of Thai people—the more affluent side of society—that grew up in big multi-family, multi-generational households, with family cooks. Through that you are exposed to a lot of these flavors that are arduous, time-consuming,

and labor-intensive.

When did you start writing the blog? Back in 2001. I think the blog [Chez Pim] came at a particular time and place. Blogging was such a new phenomenon at the time. It was my journal that just happened to be on the web.

When I started taking photos in fancy restaurants, no one was doing it, and I had this tiny Sony camera. I was really embarrassed about it, so I'd do it very quickly. But, as I wrote more about food and my blog grew, I gave interviews that got published, and suddenly I realized that all these people were reading my silly comments about a movie or a book. I told myself, "Maybe it's time to just focus on food," which I did in 2003.

So what inspired you to begin working on the other side of the camera and open your first restaurant, Kin Khao? Well, I started making jam because I was interested in working with my hands. Whenever I made a batch, I would give it to friends who were chefs and writers. [Vogue food critic] Jeffrey Steingarten actually told me, "I think you should submit your jam to the Good Food Awards. Have you heard of it?" I told him, "No, I can't, I don't even make enough!"

I had an online following at that point, so as soon as I started talking about it people would ask, "Are you selling them?" and I'd say, "Um, no. Well, wait. Maybe!" At the end of the first season, I put them online and they sold out in a day. I remember that first batch well; I posted it on Etsy. It's not like it was a runway success, but I built a small company, and by year two of the Good Food Awards, I was ready to take Jeffrey's advice. I submitted entries for two years and won both times.

People seemed to really enjoy the flavors I put together. But as good as they might think that is, I reminded myself, "You know? I'm a better Thai cook than I am a jam maker."

I looked at what's available in terms of Thai food in the U.S. There are no good restaurants. No one is using fresh ingredients. No one is really making

Right: Khao Yum, southern Thai-style tumeric rice salad, pungent herbs, seasonal vegetables, sour fruits, puffed rice & tamarind+black sesame sauce.

"Why are you using this frozen shrimp that was raised in antibiotic slush and flown here from who knows where? So I said, "If I'm going to eat and live in this country, I need to learn how to do these things myself."

things from scratch. It's not like no one knows how to cook, but nobody really uses any ingredients that I want to put in my body. No one's making curry paste and chili jam from scratch because they probably don't think they could sell it for what they'd need to make it.

Meaning it's too expensive to make? Not only too expensive, but also they think that people wouldn't know the difference. It seems like all Thai restaurants go to the same website and order the menu when they open because everybody has the same dishes. But that's not my Thai food. That's not the Thai food I grew up eating. That's not the quality I grew up eating.

This reminds me of a talk I heard about how the American conception of Thai food is really this merger of two completely different traditions: street food versus traditional home cooking. Street-food cooking tends to have Malaysian, Chinese, or other external influences and is explicitly designed for quick-fry. These can be prepared in two or three minutes because the whole idea is that they're made-to-order, to eat hot right away. And the flavors are really strong so it doesn't matter if you use good ingredients if you can't taste it, right?

Versus the home cooking you're talking about, which takes days to make and is very complex. This is the food that I do at Kin Khao. I want it to feel like you know someone in Bangkok, who has a good kitchen with cooks, and this is the food you're fed in their house.

That's a powerful image. That's the food I know, that's the food I love to eat, and that's also the food I learned to cook.

Ultimately, I learned how to cook to feed myself because when I came to the States, I looked at the food in Thai restaurants and knew that's not what I want to eat. Why are you using this frozen shrimp that was raised in antibiotic slush and flown here from who knows where? And so I said, "If I'm going to eat and live in this country, I need to learn how to do these things myself."

So every summer I would go home and set a goal—this time I'm going to learn how to make this dish. Then I'd go with people I knew who could make that dish—my aunts, our cook, other people's cooks, friends of the family—and I'd ask, "Please teach me how to make this."

It was a project of many, many years where I told myself, "Okay. I want to learn how to make *kanom jin nam prik*, and no one is going to sell it in the U.S., so if I want to eat it, I have to figure out how to make it." So that's how I learned how to cook Thai food.

Did you start with something simpler, like a pop-up? If by pop-up you mean, "Hey, would you come to dinner…?" I did dinners at home all the time with friends.

Eventually, one of those friends (who works for the company that used to own the Parc 55 hotel) called and said, "So we have a little corner at this downtown hotel that we just acquired. We want to do a restaurant, but it's not the prettiest space. It's a funky corner, it's got some issues, but it's been a Thai restaurant and we thought an Asian noodle shop or something like that could work. Do you want to open a noodle shop?"

I said, "Not a noodle shop, no, but…" It got me thinking, if I could do this in a way that I don't have to raise $2 million to open a restaurant, maybe I can give it a try? The worst thing I can do is fail, and then I go back and get a proper job. I did, and it was four years ago today that we opened.

You make it sound like such a simple process, but for most people that's quite a leap to say, "Okay, I'm going to take on this funky space and see what happens." That kind of risk-taking might not be quite so unusual in the San Francisco Bay Area, but were there any particular influences that helped you make that jump? Some friends thought it was a really brilliant idea because they loved my food, and other friends were like, "Are you sure you know what you're getting yourself into? Your dinner parties are great. Just keep doing your dinner parties."

9
3

Plah Pla Mue, charred Monterey Bay squid with a tangy+spicy seafood sauce, peanuts, cilantro.

Honestly, if I would ever make a suggestion to anyone about jumping and doing something they've never done before, the smartest thing I did was to sit down and write down a list of things I didn't know how to do. I know how to cook Thai food. I know how to cook everything on my menu, possibly better than anyone in my kitchen that's ever cooked it, including my chef de cuisine, but I don't know how to cook for 200 people a night. I understand service. I've eaten enough. I've never worked in a restaurant before. I had never even waited tables before I opened Kin Khao. It was really helpful to have a list where I was very honest with myself about the things I didn't know how to do.

That's quite a mental shift from a dinner party at home. It was a huge growth experience handing off that responsibility and realizing, "Okay, if my line cook can't make this dish, if I can't teach them how to do it, it's not going on the menu."

I've found that I hire people who generally have never cooked Thai (or Asian) food before, because breaking bad habits is much harder than instilling or teaching new ones.

Thinking about that talent pool of local chefs, how did you view the San Francisco culinary scene when you opened? Has it shifted at all in four years? I don't know if it has changed much. San Francisco has always been about really good ingredients. Maybe at a point in time it was more about ingredients than about cooking, but I think that has changed a bit. Chefs here are not afraid of cooking or of doing something with those pristine ingredients.

There was nothing local in terms of Thai cooking that was the same as Kin Khao when we opened. I would argue that there's nothing like Kin Khao anywhere in the U.S. really. And I hope it's changing. I think it's changing.

Clearly other folks would be inclined to agree since you've received accolades of many stripes, including a Michelin star for three years running. We're so limited in the space that we have, and also what we can execute, it's actually a great thing because it forces us to focus. The menu has to be tight. I can't keep throwing things at it because if I'm putting a new dish in, something has to come off.

For people who really understand that Michelin has been saying for years that they're judging food on the plates, they're not surprised that Kin Khao has a star, but then you have a certain group of people who say, "You're a Michelin starred restaurant—why do you have utensils in a cup on the table?" And I say, "Because there are a lot of dishes, you'll want to use shared spoons all the time. We're not making you share with other people."

When you opened were you hoping for those kind of accolades? I wasn't hoping for a Michelin star, no. I was just aiming for a full restaurant. Also because my ex-partner David Kinch has three Michelin stars—I've seen that it's not fun to expect certain things. "Oh, October is coming now. Is it going to be a crushing disappointment or…?" I've seen that cycle and felt that opening for critics and for stars—it's like getting into an abusive relationship. You never really know what it is that gets you a star.

The first year we got a Michelin star I started thinking, "Well, maybe now we need to make some changes in certain aspects," I just told myself, "No. We're going to make good business decisions for us because, ultimately, I'd rather have a restaurant that's full, diners that are happy, and an income, rather than try to serve some sort of nameless, faceless judge whose taste we can't predict." It's just not worth it. Ultimately, it's just that this is my food. This is how we cook it. This is what we do. Though, of course, you're worried about it. Now that you have a star, you're like, "Oh god, am I going to keep it?"

On the beverage program, you collaborated with the Bon Vivants [owners of Trick Dog] on cocktails and you also have quite an interesting wine list. How did you decide to work with them, and how is your wine list composed? I love drinking wine. I'm a

"I've found that I hire people who generally have never cooked Thai (or Asian) food before, because breaking bad habits is much harder than instilling or teaching new ones."

Som Tum Papaya Salad, spicy chili+lime+fish sauce dressing, green beans, cherry tomatoes, dried shrimp, peanuts.

wine geek. And I've been serving wine with my Thai food for a long time. We choose wines that are interesting, delicious, and priced very well. I want people to think of wine when they think Thai food. Even with wines by the glass, something we've had our servers do since we first opened is to set up an empty glass on the table, present the bottle, and pour the wine tableside, instead of pouring behind the bar and then walking a glass to a table. People start to see bottles of wine walking around the room, and they think, "Oh, maybe there's a wine list here? I should take a look," as opposed to reflexively, "I'll have a beer."

I know I love drinking cocktails, but also on my list of what I did not know how to do is make a cocktail (besides a Corpse Reviver). I've been friends with Scott Baird (founding partner of the Bon Vivants) for a while, so I invited him over for food when chef Michael Gaines and I were testing some things—and his head exploded. He said, "I really want to do this." I love Trick Dog and its cocktails are super fun, so we got the Bon Vivants involved and they designed a cocktail program and it was a great launching point for us. We do our own thing now, but it was a very good decision to get them involved at the beginning.

On your days off, where would we find you perching? I go to Rintaro a lot. It's in my neighborhood. It's on my side of town and, to me, it's like the Kin Khao of Japanese food. It's made with really, really good ingredients. It's really good cooking. But they approach it so simply. It also has the same kind of busy and bustling feel—you're basically sitting arm to arm with the next person in front of you at the yakitori line, but it's fun. I probably go to Rintaro and Piccino more often than I go anywhere because Piccino is two blocks from my loft. I can walk there and it's such simple cooking but it's delicious. Their salads and pastas are so good and I love their wine list. And they're nice people.

To what degree do you think of Kin Khao as a Thai restaurant that's elevating what Thai food should be, versus a great restaurant that happens to

cook with Thai flavors? For one thing, I don't think of myself as elevating Thai food. I'm doing it justice. For us, there will be people that come and say, "Why is your green curry thirty-something dollars as opposed to fifteen at the restaurant across the street?" "Well, because we made the curry paste this morning and the rabbit came from the same producer who sells to Saison. Have you seen the menu at Saison?"

This is what we can sell and this is what I can do to use the ingredients I want to use, cook it the way I want to cook it, and make a good business for me, my partner and my staff. There's going to be pushback. If you look in Yelp, the first thing they say is, "This is really good but Thai food shouldn't be so expensive." And I'm like, "Okay, feel free to go pay $14 for this curry paste that was made two years ago, diluted in some canned coconut milk, and then has some random frozen protein thrown in it. If you're okay with that, you should go there." We're not the restaurant you want to eat in, and I'm fine with that. I know we're not going to please everybody but obviously we've pleased enough people that we're full all the time. And I'm sure Rintaro gets the same. Mister Jiu's gets the same thing: "How do you get to charge this much for Chinese food in Chinatown?" And Brandon may tell you,"This is my food. This is what we cook with. This is the quality I'm happy with, and you can try to book a table or you can go across the street."

It's encouraging that there are so many diners who value that experience and are happy to return. Do you think you could have opened Kin Khao anywhere else? Before I opened Kin Khao, of course, I wasn't sure. [In hindsight], I think San Francisco was the perfect place for us to have a first restaurant because I know the scene very well. I know where to find good ingredients, and which farmers I can ask to grow a strange, green vegetable for us. So for me, it was a great place to have a first place. But I hope there's room for us elsewhere. I'll just leave it at that.

Does that mean you have something new in the works? We do have some

news to share. We're going to be opening a new restaurant in Japantown (SF) called *Nari* [a Thai word for woman]. It's a bigger space with a bigger kitchen, which will allow us to do even more.

Kin Khao is definitely here to stay though. If you look at Tartine, they're doing really well at Manufactory, but trust me, no matter where they go and how successful they are, they're not closing the original bakery. Kin Khao may not be in the best neighborhood—we're probably the one Michelin-starred restaurant in the world with a lady who comes in from the street occasionally and takes off her clothes (we know her by name!). But it's also my first kitchen. It's always going to have a place in my heart.

Speaking of Tartine, I have heard word of a joint project at the San Francisco airport? The airport project came about when Chad [Robertson] and Liz [Prueitt, owners of Tartine] asked to meet for dinner one day. They said, "Hey, someone approached us about this big space at the airport, and we don't want to do it alone. You interested?" I'm excited to try something fast-casual. I have ideas on what to sell, and how we want to control quality so that we make dishes the way we want. It's thrilling and terrifying, but it's a great learning opportunity and a chance to work with a couple of friends who are really good at what they do.

You also seem to be spending a lot of time in Bangkok these days. It's the craziest thing—I was recently invited to take over the kitchen at Nahm in Bangkok, which is such a tremendous opportunity. It's a chance to share my experience of Thai home cooking in an entirely new way. The old traditions of home cooking are fading and this is another way to keep them going. I feel as though I'm a link in this long chain maintained by Thai women, and if I don't help keep some of these things going, they are just going to die off.

I'll be splitting my time between Bangkok and San Francisco, which sounds kind of crazy, but I think Kin Khao will benefit from it too. I'll be bringing a lot of creative energy and new techniques back to the Bay Area with me.

—

Chef Pim Techamuanvivit.

Women Shall Inherit the Bay

Words by Carlisle Williams
Photography by Kelly Puleio

Nicole Krasinski is the matriarch of two families. When her son falls sick and she has to step away for a few days, she is acutely aware of the void this leaves in her other family at State Bird Provisions, where she is the chef-owner. "It's funny because people always ask once you have one kid, 'Are you going to have another?' and I'm like, 'I have a hundred! I have a hundred children at the restaurant! A hundred and one! I think we're good!'"

Female chefs in San Francisco have conquered many conventional metrics of accomplishment: Michelin-starred restaurants, James Beard awards, and ownership of multiple restaurants. Although these women have achieved success in the overwhelmingly male-dominated culinary field, they do not accept that the next generation should have to combat similar issues in order to be successful. Gender stereotyping, balancing a family, and finding mentors are roadblocks that leading female chefs in San Francisco are committed to removing for those that come after them.

Traci des Jardins, chef and owner of six restaurants in San Francisco including the acclaimed Jardinière and a two-time James Beard award-winner, believes that change begins with shifting perceptions of effective leadership away from traditionally male-characteristics: "I think we need to appreciate the differences between women and men. When we do, there will be greater equality. We have to stop measuring women and men as the same; we are different, as is how we approach everything. When those differences are appreciated rather than criticized, the competitive playing field will be equalized."

Restaurant kitchens in popular culture usually depict a military-style precision and deference: a group of younger chefs all cowering and replying "Yes, chef!" as a male chef yells and scowls. Female chefs, many of whom came up through the ranks in kitchens like these, have felt pressured to conform to these norms in order to be seen as leaders.

"I think people often expect male chefs to be strong and tough—if even a bit scary, and there can be pressure for female chefs to adopt these traits. To me, the reality is not about gender," said Melissa Perello, chef-owner of Michelin-starred restaurants Frances and Octavia in San Francisco. Perello has worked in the restaurant industry since high school, when she worked 40 hours per week in the kitchen at a country club. "There are simply different ways to lead. The truth is that there are plenty of tough male chefs and their female counterparts are just as tough."

Instead of continuing this tradition of a classically-male version of toughness in kitchens, many leading female chefs are consciously redefining fortitude and leadership by example in their own kitchens.

"Counterbalancing any stereotype isn't about over-correcting to prove a point," continued Perello, who named her restaurant Frances after her grandmother, who was a powerful culinary influence. "It's about adopting your own truth and personal style, and allowing that to be your voice. There is no one type of female chef and, as the conversation evolves, I hope people will see that."

In fact, female chefs not only want to expand how chefs exhibit leadership in the kitchen, but also highlight the unique ways in which women can bring alternative management and organizational approaches to a restaurant.

At The Charter Oak in St. Helena, you spot the tattooed, laser-focused chef Katianna Hong immediately: she's front and center at the enormous wood-fired cooking hearth. Hong feels passionately that historically traditional, domestic female roles help cultivate a particular brand of strong female leadership that she applies to her management of The Charter Oak kitchen. "Women run households. Women plan holidays. Women raise families. And, in the kitchen, we are one big household. We have a lot of people, a lot of personalities, and a lot of employees to care for—that requires a lot of organization. I think it's almost natural that there's a motherly figure there keeping everyone in-line and keeping the day running."

100

Chef Katianna Hong, The Charter Oak Restaurant.

The conversation on gender stereotyping must also include a discussion of intersectionality and the unique set of challenges female chefs-of-color face. Reem Assil believes that these voices add strength and dimension to the conversation.

"Being a woman of color as a chef in a heavily male-dominated industry can be daunting but, whenever I have my doubts, I think about the strong women of color I've built relationships with in this field and beyond who give me inspiration to continue my journey," said Assil, chef-owner of Oakland-based Reem's California, who was a semifinalist for the 2018 James Beard Award for Best Chef West. When we spoke, Assil was not only juggling the responsibilities of the restaurant but also preparing to give birth. She has been an outspoken advocate not only for women in the culinary industry, but also for people of color. "[Women of color] are the ones often going against the trend and speaking up for what they believe in, even when it's uncomfortable, whether it's calling out racism or sexism, or making bold decisions around how they choose to do their work."

"It's the patronizing lens of a certain type of chef-culture that continually pays lip service to the kitchens of their *nonna* (grandmother) or *babushka* and the food stalls and carts of the *abuela* (grandmother), but doesn't truly consider any of this of equal value in their own workplace," said Emma Lipp, director of food at Scribe Winery in Sonoma. Lipp had just returned from a trip to Oaxaca, Mexico, where she admired the prevalence of female chefs preparing food that they had grown over grills in the marketplaces. "You still see all-male line-ups for food festivals or high-profile chef series, or the same three token female chefs continuously."

"The rise [in voice] of the female chef is exciting because it means that we are shifting power in the industry to give voice to folks who have often been more voiceless and whose contributions [have been] overlooked," continued Assil. "We have so much to offer, not just culinarily but in our leadership. It's exciting to see how restaurants will lead with more women in charge. I imagine that workplaces will become more diverse, equitable, and be a place for folks—particularly those who haven't had a chance (women, queer folks, people of color, etc.)—to grow and be cultivated into leaders themselves."

Gabriela Cámara, chef-owner of San Francisco's Cala, located in Hayes Valley, believes that restaurants and kitchens have always been the epicenter of mixing cultures and traditions, adding, "My culinary training began with my Italian grandmother and my Mexican aunts, so it is exciting for me that more and more women are evolving their passion for cooking into full-time careers."

While women have been present in kitchens throughout history, until recently they have been widely underrepresented in terms of accolades and recognition. The San Francisco Bay Area culinary scene, with its concentration of high-caliber female chefs, has been the breeding ground for a conversation around gender issues, and actively working to change power dynamics in the industry. Each of these female chefs not only manages the everyday struggles of owning and running exceptional restaurants in a competitive city, but also commits themselves to actively advocating against gender stereotypes and the lack of female representation in the workforce, adding their voices to the national conversation.

Dominique Crenn, chef-owner of two-Michelin-starred Atelier Crenn, Petit Crenn, and the recently-opened Boutique Crenn in Salesforce Tower, is frequently highlighted as not just a top chef, but more specifically a top "female" chef. She has taken her role in stride. Crenn speaks excitedly, her French accent highlighting her passion, "We can't be complicit and complacent anymore. We have to act, we have to be a part of the change, and that's the effort. We have to continue to talk and to push. We are not there yet."

Although all of these chefs have been spurred into advocacy and the promotion of furthering opportunities in kitchens

Nicole Krasinski, State Bird Provisions.

Octavia, owned by chef Melissa Perello.

Chef Traci des Jardins, Jardinière.

for women, each has assumed the mantle in her own way.

For 13 years, des Jardins has advocated for women through her involvement with La Cocina, a nonprofit that assists low-income, female entrepreneurs by providing affordable commercial kitchen space, internships, and access to culinary job opportunities. "I am a fairly private person and have never relished the celebrity of the current chef world or how we live in a world broadcast at every moment, but I do appreciate how it leverages our ability to raise money for charities we believe in, such as La Cocina, Share Our Strength, WildAid—the list goes on. That is the silver lining of having such a high profile."

"I hope to be a part of changing the industry for today's young female chefs, to make sure they're seen as equals and treated with respect. When I look back, I'd like to think I had a part in making things better than my generation found them when we were coming up through the ranks," said Perello.

Krasinski looks to herself as an example for the women in her restaurant. "As a business owner, a woman, and a mom, I cherish being the example. Over half of our staff is female, and 70 percent of our management team is women. I often say, 'Look! You can do this. It's possible. It's not out of reach. If you really want it, there are certainly compromises and sacrifices.' But I can't imagine doing anything else."

Like Krasinski, Perello fosters the next generation of female chefs through mentorship and guidance. "I hope to be a part of changing the industry for today's young female chefs, to make sure they're seen as equals and treated with respect. When I look back, I'd like to think I had a part in making things better than my generation found them when we were coming up through the ranks," said Perello.

Kelly Mariani of Scribe knows first-hand how mentorship can shepherd and inspire new female chefs. "I feel lucky to have worked for a female chef that is widely respected by everyone. Alice Waters has a grace and confidence about her that is reassuring. She knows her stuff. Most importantly, she believes in her cooks. Working for her allowed for space to be mentored in the kitchen, and gain my own confidence on the way, without passive aggression or judgement. I think that is a tough line to walk as a female chef."

"The SFBA is a particularly extraordinary community to cook in because it is home to so many of the nation's top female chefs. This is one of the things that inspires me most about working in San Francisco," said Cámara. "It's an honor to be part of this tradition and I look forward to watching this legacy continue with future generations of female chefs."

"We are here, we've been here for a long time, and we are here to stay," added Crenn. "What excites me is that the conversation has started with everyone— and now we are building the momentum of the national conversation on female rights. I think that's going to bring a new perspective in [our] industry but also to a lot of other industries."

For centuries, female chefs had to not only be technically great chefs, but also had to manage the politics of being female in a male-dominated profession. Although they acknowledge that gendered issues still exist, this strong, vocal group of female chefs based in the SFBA is using its voices and its restaurants to create environments that encourage success based on merit.

—

A Hog Island State of Mind

Words by Celia Sack
Photography by Daniela Velasco

Summer, 2000. "Meet me at Hog Island. They let me keep my boat there." At the invitation of a friend, my girlfriend Paula and I take our dog and race up to the coast of Tomales Bay from San Francisco. It usually takes an hour and a half, but with my foot on the accelerator, it's closer to an hour. Parking is where you can find it, usually snug up against a curve in the road, where Highway One bends along the shore.

The muddy stench of low tide wafting up to mix with oyster and clam shells in water baths, along with the constant plop of shells tossed by workers after being cleaned, is essentially the soundtrack of Hog Island Oyster Company. Jane's standing in her wellies, and says, "I'll walk out and pull it up so you don't have to sink into the mud." That English accent. That fair complexion. Those sky-blue eyes. Paula and I sigh as she confidently strides into the mudflats to retrieve her little aluminum boat. We let her take each of our hands and direct us into the shell, and then we convince Tessa, our dog, to jump aboard. Halfway across the Bay, she points out the real Hog Island, covered with trees, imposing with steep granite. Tessa spots a shiny black seal and tries to jump out after it— we pull her back. The seal seems to wink at us before heading back under the cold waves.

Paddling over to the other side we discover a beach to ourselves, and the ruins of an abandoned house that once belonged to the last resident allowed to live in this national park. We clamber around the rotting decks, peering through broken windows at the remains of a life. A worn out, stained mattress. A lamp on its side. A typewriter, perhaps? It's hard to say. We lie on the beach in the sun, and become better acquainted with our friend. I ask about London. "Did you really play cards with Diana?"

Back at Hog Island's picnic tables, we open a mesh bag of small, sweet Miyagi oysters pulled from one of the tanks. It's just the three of us there on this bright afternoon, the sun glinting off the water. "You've never shucked an oyster? Let me show you how." Jane cups her gloved

hand around mine, guides the oyster knife between the lips of the shell, pops the top shell off. "Now you try." Suck the seawater out. Tip the creamy bivalve into your mouth. Throw the empty shell with abandon onto the ground, where hundreds of others lie.

Summer, 2005. "Can you pick up the oysters?" Paula and I own a home in Tomales now, just 15 minutes north of Hog Island Oyster Co. It's our tenth anniversary, and we're throwing a party with a caterer, a bartender—the whole nine yards. I'm picking up the oysters. Things have changed at the oyster company. There's a new parking lot now. It's covered in oyster shells, attended by valets. Lines have gotten longer too. "100 Miyagis and 100 Kumamotos, please." "And a bag of littleneck clams for a linguine I'll make tomorrow." "No ice, I'm just up the road." I zig and zag back up Highway One, past stately hawks on their telephone poles, cows grazing on brown grass, fog creeping back across the Bay toward Inverness. There's no traffic, save slowing for a covey of quail to cross the road. I'll show the caterer how to shuck the oysters; I've been doing it for years now. Ten years is a long time to be together—something to celebrate. They say happy relationships take work, but that's not always true. We've had way more of our ups than downs—an unfair share, some might say. Our friends laze in the grass back at the house, nibbling cheese from nearby Cowgirl Creamery, catching up on gossip. Champagne and oysters, toasts to more years of happiness and good fortune.

Summer, 2015. "We're having a party at Hog Island! Bunch of lesbians. Join us!" Two friends have fallen in love. They live in New York, but are spending their summer vacation at a rental house next to Hog Island Oyster Co. Couples converge on the picnic tables that now require reservations and rental fees. There's even a faux boat shack where, for a fee, they'll shuck the oysters for you. I'm trying not to be all "in the old days…" about it, but here we are." My friends are grilling sausages, shucking oysters, and mixing a huge Caesar salad at the table—laughing, flirting, yelling to be heard, shaking our

hands. "Have we met before?" We bring beer and wine; the tables are littered with bottle caps, half-eaten bread. Paper plates and napkins flutter away to crowded, neighboring tables. Someone's kid runs from table to table, stopping to pet the dogs. Our new dog, Jolene, licks out the empty shells tossed down.

Summer, 2016. By the next summer, our friends tell us one of the longtime couples we met broke up, and now they're fighting over custody of their kids. We still have another party, but there's more tension in the air; our friends needle and nag each other, turning away to separate conversations. They'll break up by the following summer, and someone else's party will reserve their table, slurp their oysters, joust over a keg of beer rolled over shells to the edge of the Bay.

Fall, 2017. "I'll go get the oysters before they run out." It's Paula's 60th birthday, and friends and family will be at our house in a few hours. The line is short, but it's all big men buying endless sacks of large oysters to grill at a tailgate party. "More ice." "Better get a few more bags of oysters." "I'll throw them in the truck." "Got any hot sauce?" they ask. To each his own. Some people like their oysters cooked—big, meaty, and drowned in barbecue sauce, all seawater evaporated away. I prefer subtler, dainty oysters with just a squirt of lemon. Maybe some Champagne mignonette. But mostly in the nude, still alive in their brine when I suck them down. Finally, my turn to order. "150 small Kumamotos. No ice—I live just up the road." "Sure, I'll take the locals discount." Gonna be a hot day; October's always like this. "Having a birthday party—my wife's 60th. Yes, I've been coming here over twenty years now. And I'll be back."

—

Reconsidering the Authentic

Words by Leigh Biddlecome
Photography by Molly DeCoudreaux

According to the philosopher-scholar Michael Walzer, a person is considered to be "inauthentic" when she has "failed to live up to [her] principles."

In the food world, the word "authentic" has become both a charged touchstone and a term mostly emptied of recognizable meaning. Charges of "inauthenticity" are hurled at restaurants and cafes in the course of online reviews from the masses, whilst establishments try to pre-empt criticisms by inserting "authentic" into press releases, across mission statements, and onto menus. The result is a confusing proliferation of a term that despite—or perhaps because of—its frequent use lacks a settled understanding. Like so many other buzzwords of our time connected to consumption (consider "curate" another), its use seems more often related to a desire to be seen by others as knowing the fashionable word, rather than expressing a precise meaning.

Perhaps the logical inverse of Walzer's description—that is, authenticity means living up to a set of principles—is the first step in the search for a more elemental understanding of the concept. But what are these principles, and, in the domain of food, who gets to decide them? Perhaps more critically in San Francisco right now, how does the rise of an authenticity-obsessed culture relate to a parallel increase in wealth and racial homogeneity?

………..

I should admit that these questions have also evolved from the experience of moving back to the San Francisco Bay Area from Europe several years ago, after nearly a decade away, and discovering a city that seemed to be steadily flattening in every sense except topographically. A sameness in consumer culture, industry, and ethos alongside an increasing economic inequality was—simply put—disturbing. What emerges is that questions of authenticity are not just relevant to the city's cultural history, but integral to any consideration of its growth.

Italian and Italian-American cuisine in the SFBA provide a surprisingly apt touchpoint, with their reflections of multiple waves of immigrants and the changing demographics of the region. Questions of authenticity also become particularly charged when speaking of a cuisine that has both an "assimilated" version (i.e. Italian-American) and an "original" version (experienced either in Italy, or, in restaurants outside of Italy claiming to recreate the original cuisine).

The first wave of immigrants from Italy to San Francisco arrived in the mid-19th century and built up the neighborhood near the docks, dominating the fishing industry within 50 years. Today, Little Italy draws throngs of tourists to its Italian-American red-sauce joints and to a shrinking group of old, Italian-American businesses. One of these is Liguria Bakery, occupying a corner-shop across from the edifice of Saints Peter and Paul Catholic Church. These days the bakery has cut back its production to variations on a single theme: focaccia. Founded by the current-owner Michael Soracco's grandfather in 1911, its name references the northern Italian region where focaccia is a mainstay, and hints at San Francisco's unique position within America as a center for immigration from the north of Italy (Chicago and New York were settled by mostly southern, rather than northern, Italians).

Liguria Bakery is spare inside: tile floors, a couple of chairs, and mostly-empty white shelves. When I walk in on a Tuesday morning, there are a few locals sitting around with Michael's sister Mary, and their mother, Josephine, the co-owner, who preside over the counter chatting about another neighborhood business. The mom-and-pop feel and the casual, social atmosphere reminds me immediately of Italy, as does the yeasty, olive-oil fragrance coming from the back of the bakery. Looking at the menu, though, the "jalapeño and cheese" focaccia is startling, amidst the four or five other classics spelled out in white plastic letters on a black felt board ("plain," "olive," "onion"). The Soraccos explain that the jalapeño focaccia was an innovation for Cinco de Mayo one year, which proved to be so popular that it never left the menu. So "jalapeño," with its very non-Italian "ñ" and domestic

Chef Michael Tusk.

116

cheese topping, remains unapologetically there on the menu, a subtle reference to the traditionally strong Latino influence on the culture and cuisine of San Francisco.

A different story of cross-cultural adoption can be found at Dianda's Italian-American Pastry Company in the Mission District. The bakery, on the ground floor of a beige, architecturally unremarkable building, is one of a couple of businesses that recall the neighborhood's earlier days as an Italian enclave—although today the Mission is better known for having been the heart of San Francisco's Latino culture for much of the 20th century. The neighborhood has also been the site of battles over aggressive gentrification over the last 10 years, as new residents —many with tech salaries—have displaced large numbers of the Latino community.

Dianda's tells an older story of neighborhood transition: the left display case is packed with traditional Northern Italian cookies—*biscotti, panforte,* and *brutti ma buoni*; and on the right, a brightly hued line of their now-famous *tres leches* cakes. On a Saturday afternoon, the animated Spanish of a long line of customers floods the space, an altogether captivating, unexpected blend of a small Italian town and Mexico City. The current trio of owners, who started out as bakers under the Dianda family and took over in 2004, are two Mexican-Americans and a self-described "Jewish guy from Brooklyn." Not a single Italian works for Dianda's anymore—a fact that might scare off the Italian purist, but otherwise strikes me as a fascinating example of a successful transfer of artisanship from one immigrant culture to another. It also happens to be patronized nearly exclusively by the neighborhood's older residents and Latino population.

But, ultimately, what to make of the "japaleño focaccia" and *tres leches* cake alongside the Italian *panforte*? What of the adoption of Mexican flavors into the Italian repertoire—and in the case of Dianda's, the adoption of an Italian business by two Mexicans and a "Jewish guy?" When considered within the American urban context, this culinary

mingling strikes me as almost banal in its literal embodiment of our beloved melting pot story. For San Francisco's new, young, tech-elite demographic, however, I worry that placing cuisine within its local and historical context will get lost amidst an almost obsessive, purist's drive to find "the authentic." For this group, authenticity is based on the principle of being "true to the original," i.e. the "version from the country of origin." The average member of this demographic bases dining decisions on meticulous online research. She is likely to have enough income to have visited Italy as a tourist at least once, she seeks to replicate this memory—not some disfigured Italian-American version. Pair this with the very real phenomenon of an increasingly *un*-diverse city (and I mean this both in terms of homogeneity of mindset as well as race and class), and you end up with a culture that prizes "unadulterated" cuisine—while oblivious to the fact that the conditions that have been central to creating new culinary-culture combinations are being sucked right out from under us.

. . . .

Stuck in these demoralizing thoughts, I get in touch with two chefs who I think might offer some alternative principles for authenticity, and consequently help us develop a theory for how we might inspire the public to a different approach. I'm especially curious as to how the city's newer generation of Italian restaurants position themselves between the principles of Italian and Northern-Californian cuisines. My hunch is that these two chefs—Matthew Accarrino of SPQR and Michael Tusk of Cotogna—at the very least complicate the belief that "the more classic Italian dishes on the menu, the more authentic the restaurant."

Chef Accarrino of the "Italian-inspired," Michelin-starred SPQR comes from an Italian-American family in New Jersey, and has also spent significant time working with and visiting family members across Italy. When we first meet, amidst the bustle of prep for dinner service, he's energetic, direct, and quickly informs me that his approach to the idea of authenticity is one with

Cotogna Restaurant.

a certain skepticism, even playfulness. Many of the Italian names on the menu are intentionally framed in quotations, like his "garnet yam gnocchi with a beef and black garlic 'bolognese.'" The quotes acknowledge the Asian influence of black garlic, but he also reminds me (only half-kidding), that "you're not eating it on a square in Italy." Striking a more serious note, he explains that Italian food is deeply linked with a particular time and place—the work of generations, using almost exclusively what they had close at hand. Importing Italian ingredients to California to recreate Italian dishes would be contrary to that spirit, he believes. Instead, he would rather stray from that particular version of authenticity in order to "distill experiences and flavors into a different form." This distillation still is very much in line with Italian gastronomic philosophy—working with *materie prime* (raw ingredients) from local cheese makers, farmers, and charcutiers. Accarrino's reluctance to enter into a reductive debate on his relative authenticity (or not) refocuses the discussion.

Chef Tusk of Cotogna greets me mid-afternoon in his neighboring restaurant, Quince, with the slightly harried look of someone who's coming directly from several meetings and a lunch service. He quickly softens as the substance of our talk starts to mirror the menu of Cotogna itself: anecdotes of his formative experiences in Italy involving particular ingredients alternate with rumination on what it means to cook them within a Northern Californian context. He recalled a trip to Modena in which he was invited to dinner by a *nonna* figure who simply popped out to her backyard to pick some nettles to add to a pasta course. Admitting "a soft spot for nettles," this spurred Tusk to find a way to bring the wild nettles that grow around Fresh Run Farm onto the menu at Cotogna—currently starring in a *sformata* antipasto and the nettle *tortelli*. There is humility in his desire to go constantly "to the source" in Italy in order to learn as much as possible—but also an openness when back in his kitchen to be creative with what is at hand: "balancing innovation and tradition," as he puts it. He adds, "a dish isn't authentic just

because you're copying it line for line; it's more about the essence of it. Does it *remind* you in its immediacy of that original taste experience?" So he might start with a desire to recreate the Venetian sense of being "surrounded by water" (befitting San Francisco), but instead of making a *spaghetti alle vongole*, he would recreate the sensibility of that Italian dish by using a SFBA-native shellfish paired with a house-made pasta—a move he admits came only with time, confidence, and a certain "honesty," as he quietly puts it. Concern with both the tangible (raw ingredients) as well as the more ethereal ("essences" and "taste experiences," as he says) are indicative of Tusk's sophisticated understanding of how the chef-artist might eschew the more reactionary version of the authentic in favor of principles that reference multiple traditions—in this case, from Northern California and Italy.

....

If current trends of taste and demographics continue in San Francisco, it is conceivable that the spontaneous, quirky merging of various culinary cultures (of the jalapeño-focaccia variety) will cease to exist unless engineered for concept restaurants (i.e., sushi-burrito chains). And while this outcome is not on the same level as the grave, concurrent issues of evictions and displacement, it is at our own peril that we disregard our fixation on authenticity. As any employee of Facebook or Google is well aware, consumer purchasing choices betray a set of values and corresponding political beliefs. If these choices privilege authenticity in its simplistic form—favoring the "pure original"—then I believe these thought patterns are not merely unsophisticated, but when considered within the context of current demographic shifts in the city, they edge disconcertingly close to a politics of homogeneity.

All of this is on my mind as I contemplate leaving this city, which has moved further and further in a direction that troubles me in its increasing economic inequality (and, simultaneously, towards sameness in its consumer culture). In the meantime, to

combat the unsettling obsession with the authentic as "fidelity to a pure original," I would encourage us to imagine a different set of principles upon which to base the term: say, fidelity to an "essence," as Chef Tusk might suggest, or fidelity to a taste memory or emotion. And when forging new territory between multiple traditions, then consider discarding the concept entirely—especially in those unlikely of circumstances when *tres leches* shares the shelf with *biscotti*.

—

Caramelle with fresh run farm broccoli; Cotogna.

Meyer lemon linguini, abalone 'alfredo,' American bottarga and garlic chips, SPQR.

Left: Mushroom and root vegetable 'stufato', SPQR.
Right: Chef Matthew Accarrino, SPQR.

The Phoenix of Los Gatos

Interview and photography by
Adam Goldberg

Where the line blurs between Silicon Valley and the Santa Cruz Mountains, you'll find Manresa, tucked away in the tony suburb of Los Gatos. Manresa opened in 2002, just after the dot-com bubble popped. At that time, very few high-end restaurants—Chez Panisse, French Laundry—in California were serving local, farm-to-table dishes in a fine-dining format. Behind the scenes, a young David Kinch was learning from these trailblazers, posting frequently to online forums like eGullet and experimenting in the kitchen at his newly opened restaurant Manresa. He also began traveling extensively—to France, Spain, and Japan—bringing aspects of his favorite foreign dishes back home. Diners who followed his evolution quickly became loyalists.

Though much has changed since then, today, Kinch applies the same curiosity to preparing exceptionally high-quality, locally-procured ingredients such as abalone and foie gras with his trademark personality and astuteness. Here, we hear from chef Kinch on how his three-Michelin-starred restaurant is staying the test of time, how fine-dining has been democratized, and how detaching his personal life from the success of his restaurant is, perhaps, one of the best decisions he's ever made.

Left: Chef David Kinch.

What is Manresa? How did the concept start? Why did you pick Los Gatos?
I had never been to California. I was working in New York as a young cook in my twenties, and halfway through my tenure there, the owner was invited by a sake distributor to go on a junket to Japan. He went and came back a transformed man. Many know that experience; you go to Japan and your eyes are opened about the ways things can be done. After he returned, he changed the direction of the restaurant. I bought it hook, line, and sinker. I was fascinated by it. In terms of my own personal education, I then realized that I wanted to work in Japan more than anything else, so instead of going to work in Europe or continuing working in New York, I decided to spend some time working in Japan.

Six months before a gig started [in Japan], I had some time to kill. My parents had just moved out to California, so I went to visit them.

I started working at a winery, Mount Eden Vineyard, which is in the Santa Cruz mountains. I had no idea at the time, but it was literally right down the road from Manresa, in Saratoga. I remember first getting off the plane in California. It was 72 degrees—in February. I had left New York and the gray slush. I recall thinking, "You've got to be kidding me. Really?" The mythology of California, the weather and everything—it hit me full in the face.

Japan did not last as long as I had wanted it to. When I left I didn't want to return to New York. On a whim, I decided to stay in California. I worked in San Francisco for a while, and I started making plans for my own restaurant. Then I went back to Europe and worked for two years, doing a series of stages. When I came back, I opened my first restaurant. It was bistro-like: 30 seats, loud, and noisy. It was in Saratoga, which is down the road from Los Gatos. It was busy from day one. We were open for about seven years, but I got really tired of the small kitchen. I was a driven cook and wanted to do ambitious food; that would involve a relocation.

That's when we found the space that is currently Manresa. It was a dilapidated building that had been a restaurant called the Village House, and it was run by ladies from a charity organization, the Ming Quong. It closed and was left vacant for 10 years. [When we took possession], there was only half a roof and graffiti-covered walls. I fell in love with the location, so we bought the building and moved in July of 2002. Manresa celebrated its 15th anniversary last year.

You're probably one of the most well-traveled chefs that I know. Do you think that travel has had a strong impact on your cooking? For me, along with reading books, it is the singular source of inspiration for what we do. When you travel, you have an opportunity to smell and taste things. Of course, you visit the restaurants of your peers, the restaurants that are trendy and that people write about, and the places that you hear about elsewhere. I also like going off of the beaten paths. One of my favorite things to do is visit a place that I haven't been to before. Usually because I'm jet-lagged and up early, I visit the market. Visiting a market, a central market, in a place you've never been before tells you what you need to know about where you are and what people eat and buy. It's really fascinating. I get a lot of inspiration from visiting these markets—from talking to the people who work the stands, the consumers, and, of course, by eating. I travel a lot but there are many places I haven't been. I have a bucket list, but it's tough for me to ignore old favorites and the urge to revisit places.

What are some of your other favorite places? France. Call me old-fashioned or out of touch, but I love going to France.

When you're planning a trip to a new city, what's your process for compiling that list? I use Michelin as a reference. I don't treat it as a bible, but I certainly treat it as a good source. I contact people I know who live there for recommendations. I look for a balance of trendy and traditional places. For example, my favorite restaurant to eat at in Copenhagen is Schønnemann.

Into the Garden.

It's a traditional, open-faced sandwich (*smørrebrød*) joint that serves aquavit.

I know some people who go to cities and eat in Michelin-starred restaurants just to check it off a list. Obviously social media has had a strong impact on destination dining. How do you think that's impacted fine dining, or what you've seen here at the restaurant? Ten years ago, people didn't take photographs of food. Now you stand out if you don't. I don't have a beef with it, as long as it doesn't interfere with the surrounding tables. I understand the impact and the appeal of social media in all the food that's out there, but it's a lot of information. I don't want to call it garbage, but there is a lot of debris floating around. And it can be a deterrent to your own ideas. You're so bombarded by ideas, colors, and dishes— visual images—that it's tough to dig out and create your own style. It becomes almost a pollution of sorts.

You get older and people say that you start to lose your memory, or you lose your ability a little. To some extent, it might be true. But I had this conversation with someone who said people lose memory at an earlier age nowadays, and much of it has to do with the fact that it's just simply too much information for the conscience and the awareness. It's harder to remember things because there's so much to remember nowadays. So I try to stay away from it because you see so many things you'd like to do, or how they did it and that sort of thing. You begin to lose track of your own vision. I try to take a step back. I think it's good for some things, but I'd rather go to the restaurant and eat and experience the dishes—the touch, the smell, the ambience of the restaurant, the service— as opposed to seeing the 18 courses listed in an Instagram feed or something like that. It kills it. It feeds into that notch-on-the-belt impulse of "I've got to go to these places," and it destroys the sense of discovery and the element of surprise, which is still important when going to a nice restaurant.

It's this double-edged sword. On the one hand, you can see the menu from any restaurant in the world immediately; you just open Instagram. You can virtually eat there. There's less of the element of surprise. Do you think that seeking out these fine-dining restaurants has become less special as a result of this information overload? Short answer, yes. The good news is that there's been this giant democratization of fine dining. Fine dining was an elitist concept. It is what you did on a birthday, or an anniversary, or what you did if you were a really rich person. And the quality of cooking that you can get at different price ranges is miles ahead of the way it used to be. Dishes that you had 25 years ago in fine-dining restaurants are middle-of-the-road right now. It's now a golden age of dining. There is a parallel in the wine world. The best wines made in all of history have been made in the last 35 to 40 years. Technology has changed the understanding of grapes, from how they work to where they grow. Education, cross-pollination of ideas, people sharing information, and interconnectivity have all changed, from Burgundy to New Zealand—the list goes on. Wines are healthier, they're better balanced, and they offer lots of pleasure. People drink differently now.

> "Food has gotten so much better, but it has become so much the same."

The downside is that there's ubiquitousness in the wines. It's the same thing with food. Food has gotten so much better, but it has become so much the same. We've lost uniqueness, and that's why I think there is such an emphasis placed on creativity as a supreme value [today], which I think is a really big mistake. The supreme values are taste and pleasure. Is creativity part of the mix? Yes. But creativity as supreme quality, so that people stand out, so that people perceive you as being unique? It feeds into social media and things looking good, but not necessarily tasting good. But it doesn't matter because you're not tasting it, you're just looking at it. It feeds on itself.

That's the kind of stuff I'm trying to step back from. I want to follow my instincts: the things that influence me, my personal experiences, my travel, what I read, my interactions with my cooks, the collaborations with my staff, and the things that I don't like. And I want those to be the major drivers of Manresa's future direction, as opposed to trying to be trendy or trying to set myself apart. I think we do things that are different, that are unique, but it's not because of reading feeds. I think it's bred from within.

You mentioned that you're the happiest that you've been in the last couple of years? We had the fire, which was a catalyst for many different things. We reopened in January of 2015. It was a chance to re-evaluate not only everything that we did at the restaurant, but also to revisit the guest experience. Usually you don't have time for these [considerations], but all of a sudden we had the time. There was also time for personal reflection on what was important. I made a big mistake in attaching my personal life, and livelihood to that of the restaurant, which a lot of chefs do. They become their restaurant. So when the restaurant burned, a part of me burned as well. And I was in a pretty bad place. I realized I couldn't do that anymore. I had to find a degree of separation and a certain level of balance. Because if I didn't, it was going to severely affect my health. It affected the way I dealt with people, relationships, and everything else that goes on in life besides your work life.

As a chef, and as an ambitious chef, everything I have ever done has been devoted to being the best cook I could possibly be, and creating the best experience I could possibly create. And I had to give that up. I had to find that balance between health and happiness, being satisfied in the work, and leading my team. It was a hard thing to do, but I accomplished it. I feel healthier and happier in my interactions with people. But more importantly—the restaurant is better than ever because of that decision. Because I'm not devoting every waking moment, whether it's positive or negative, and channeling it towards the restaurant. I'm just channeling good, strong energies to it when I want to or feel it needs to happen. It's like working smarter instead of working more.

We reopened after the fire with this mindset and, after 10 years of two stars, we received the third star immediately after. We've had a series of people working at the restaurant who are some of the best employees we've ever had. The restaurant gets better and better every year. That makes me very happy. But, I've learned to take a step back. I go on vacation. We even close two nights a week. It all helps. It was a huge reset button, and it didn't happen overnight.

The menu became more concise. Have the dishes also become healthier? We've always been fish, shellfish, vegetable, and fruit-oriented. We've offered meat dishes, but they tend to be fairly light-to-medium-bodied, almost feminine in nature. They tend to be colorful. There hasn't been a dramatic change. I have had a great interest in revisiting classical cuisine, mostly because it's completely out of fashion, and that's what attracts me to it. You can't Instagram flavor, and sauces offer a lot of pleasure. Our food is very contemporary, but we work hard to add this classical element.

Can you give me an example? Yes, there's an intense depth of flavor in a classic bouillabaisse [a Provençal seafood stew], in terms of aromatics and everything that goes into it. In ours we use dried squid and dried scallops. We take bream bones and salt them for 24 hours, then we air-dry them for a couple days. Next we smoke them, so the bones are two weeks old before we make a fumet from them, and that's not classical. Those are the steps that we've taken to build up this classical foundation. You don't know that all of that is in there, but it adds an element of flavor that makes it distinct from classical food.

Have your own experiences as a diner impacted the format of the menu? Yes. We're taking dishes off the menu. I want to create a two-and-a-half to three-hour experience for guests. I think that's the limit. Even for me, it's hard to spend three hours sitting still. I want the moment to be magical. You don't want people to strain to hit the finish line. In the frantic world we live in today, two-and-a-half to three hours is a lot to ask of people.

Now, can I go sit down at a dinner for five hours? If I'm there with great friends, and it's a special occasion, and it's in a wonderful place, I could be there all day, but those meals are the exception.

I love to eat. I still love to come to work. It gets harder and harder at my age to come to work and do the service, but I still love coming to work, and I still love to dine.

Tell me about the Vegetable Garden dish. The Vegetable Garden has been on the menu since the beginning of the relationship with Love Apple Farm, which was in 2006.

It was a dish that went through many phases until it became known. It was essentially a fancy salad. But it was a dish that was representative of the relationship between Love Apple Farm and Manresa. The rule was that everything that was on the plate had to be from Love Apple. And there was one of everything, with anywhere from 45 to 60 different things on it. Was it based on the Gargouillou [an iconic, garden-inspired dish by the French chef Michel Bras]? Yes, of course, just like a million other dishes around the planet. But, for me, it was different because it was site-specific. It was about the farm.

When we came back from the fire, everything was different. The menu was different except for the Garden because I was told, "We can't change the Garden." After the fire, I realized that the Garden was dated. We were doing all these new things, this reincarnation of Manresa after the fire, this rising of Manresa, and the one dish that we felt that we couldn't change was holding us back. We took it off the menu, and I thought, "There has to be a new incarnation for it." It became a warm ravioli dish with a lot of greens. It was a chicory root ravioli.

The relationship with Love Apple Farm ended when the farmer retired. So we've gone back to farmer's markets. There's another small farm that we work with exclusively, which is mostly botanicals, flowers, greens, and more of the lighter stuff, but it's a relationship that we don't trumpet anymore.

"Giving a shit is something you can't teach people."

Sometimes it feels like other restaurants are stuck on autopilot, but I don't feel that at Manresa, and that's something that I always like about coming here. Is that a conscious thing? Giving a shit is something you can't teach people. We found people who were young, eager, and who cared. I'll always value someone who buys into our vision. You can't teach people to care. If people care, I can show them what I want and, hopefully, create an environment for them in which to excel. We don't have much turnover at the restaurant. That's pretty special. But our rule—especially for people who come into contact with guests—is to make direct eye contact. Your smile must be genuine. If you can't do that, you can't work here. We all know what a fake smile is, and we accept it because we know, cynically, it's a transactional thing. But people know a genuine smile. So if you make direct eye contact, and your smile is genuine, we're halfway there in terms of the hospitality. People feel that. They may not be able to put their finger on what it is, but when they leave the restaurant, they're going to be like, "That was really great."

—

Savory Bavarois of Sea Urchin.

Counter Intelligence

Words by Andréa Morrissette
Photography by Daniela Velasco

The release of the 2018 Michelin Guide marked a shift in the American restaurant paradigm. Overnight, the San Francisco Bay Area was upgraded to having seven three-star restaurants—the most in the country—dethroning New York as the country's awarded epicenter for fine dining. While Michelin's highest honor remains the holy grail for some, a new guard of pedigreed chefs and entrepreneurial restaurateurs in the SFBA are ditching fine dining to embrace an entirely different concept. They call it "fast-fine" dining, describing establishments that offer high-quality ingredients and ambiance at a fraction of the price of fine dining, without the assembly line nature of fast-casual spots like Chipotle. In the SFBA, fast-fine dining provides the city's swelling population of busy professionals quick and relatively affordable dining experiences worthy of their tastes: counter service in stylish restaurants serving food made from conscientiously-sourced ingredients.

"This is how people want to dine now," says Charles Bililies, founder and CEO of Souvla, San Francisco's mini-empire of Greek fast-fine dining. Before forging his own path to open his first restaurant in 2014, Bililies worked at both The French Laundry and Michael Mina. His experience in some of the world's top restaurants quickly taught him that fine dining was not a lucrative business model, and full-service restaurants were generally a financial drain.

"As I was considering Souvla's product and menu, I was also thinking how can I take all of the touch points and standards of my fine-dining experience and distill them down to where you can order from the counter," says Bililies. A light bulb went off and he set forth to modernize the gyro with a "chef's treatment."

Walking into a number of the SFBA's fast-fine restaurants, whether during the bustling lunch service, or in the date-night hours, it's difficult to pinpoint the difference from a proper full-service restaurant. "Distinctions we've made at Souvla boil down to when you're dining and it looks, feels, and acts like a full-service restaurant; you almost don't realize you ordered at the counter because everything else around you—the fixtures, the furniture, the materials, the lighting, the artwork, the florals—feels like you're in a full-service restaurant," Bililies says.

Charming interiors evoking distant foreign locales are one of the hallmarks of fast-fine's appeal. With its bright Trinidadian tile, antique lamp posts and turquoise accents, Media Noche, a Cuban restaurant in San Francisco's Mission district, is nothing short of an Instagrammer's paradise. Co-owners Jessie Barker and Madelyn Markoe brought their travels through Havana to life with artfully-rendered interiors by designer Hannah Collins. "There is something about the aesthetic [of Media Noche] that compels people to take photos and post them—and I think that we are able to transport them to somewhere exotic when they're eating," Markoe says.

The importation and modernization of global cuisines and dishes isn't new territory for restaurants, but the sense of urgency to introduce new casual concepts to the SFBA as a result of seeing an opportunity in the marketplace to make a quick profit and ride the coattails of this trend is what has savvy restaurateurs thinking internationally. Ben Koenig, owner of Heritage Eats in Napa, wrote the business plan for his restaurant during his travels abroad, inspired by the flavorful street food of the Middle East, Southeast Asia, and India. "I thought, let's try to layer in some fine-dining elements and try and speak to the culture of food, the heritage of food, the history of food in a fast-casual interpretation," Koenig says.

The entrepreneurial spirit of the fast-fine movement encourages chefs to see an opportunity in the marketplace, and to take a chance to bring their vision to fruition. "I knew that this town was in need of something even more casual, but with diverse flavors outside of French, Italian, or American," says Chef Anita Cartagena. She came to the SFBA from the kitchens of Chicago, inspired to ultimately open Protéa, her airy, Yountville restaurant, after a life-changing

meal at The French Laundry several years prior. "I knew exactly when I came here that we would serve artisan sandwiches, global rice bowls—everything from ramen to curries—Chinese, Thai, Korean. But the baseline for everything is Caribbean, specifically Puerto Rican. I love Puerto Rican food and grew up in the kitchen with my grandmother and my mother and wanted to bring that here."

After cutting his teeth in the kitchens of AQ and One Market, and perfecting his menu at pop-up dinners and music festivals, Culinary Institute of America-trained Guy Eshel opened Sababa as a nod to his childhood memories of vibrant Israeli street food. Keeping true to the roots of Middle Eastern kiosks and food stands, he took a more chef-driven approach in the kitchen, using fresh ingredients to make his baked pita, falafels, and sauces from scratch. "I think San Francisco does fast-fine well because we have a great food scene," says Eshel. "We have super-talented chefs with fine-dining backgrounds that want to open their own spots, but are realistic about the economics of opening a full-service restaurant."

The standards for food quality aren't just kitchen concerns, but are equally driven by the expectations of diners. "People in the SFBA have really high standards for food but they don't always have the time—or the money—to go out to a fancy dinner," says Allison Hopelain. "So an easier, cheaper option that still maintains quality is a good fit." Hopelain, along with Russell Moore, makes up the dynamic couple behind Oakland's popular Camino restaurant and new fast-fine spot, The Kebabery. They opened The Kebabery in Oakland's mostly residential Longfellow neighborhood as a way to follow up on Camino's success with something fun and more flexible. "We have a lot of crossover between The Kebabery and Camino customers— they are very different experiences and commitments, but the food is made with the same care."

Similarly, Chefs Evan and Sarah Rich of the inventive, Michelin-starred Rich Table opted for a more casual approach for their second eatery, RT Rotisserie—this time, taking inspiration from themselves as working parents. "We are our own demographic," admits Sarah Rich. "We love Rich Table and wish we could eat there everyday, but we don't always have the luxury of sitting down for a dinner with multiple courses. We wanted to open a restaurant that served food as delicious as Rich Table, but in a more casual manner. Somewhere that a busy parent or working professional could come in and pick up a delicious meal without having to put much effort into dinner."

Fast-fine dining's economizing of time and budget complements the busy lifestyles of SFBA inhabitants and resonates with their need for value and quality. "The standard restaurant is falling behind due to the changing dining habits of the SFBA," says Marko Sotto, owner of Barzotto, the Mission's popular fast-fine pasta bar. "Not everyone can afford a $100 meal every night, but a lot of Bay Area residents don't cook for themselves. They want a place to go that is delicious, quick, and hip, but with a price point that doesn't leave them with sticker shock."

For Dabba's CEO Andy Mercer and Chef Walter Abrams (formerly of The French Laundry), pushing culinary boundaries to create borderless recipes combining fresh, local ingredients and healthy spices sourced from around the world was integral to their initial business plan. "Our vision is to offer beautifully made food not just to the lucky few, but to thousands of people each day for under $20—with a wait of less than five minutes," says Mercer.

Fast-fine is on the move towards growth and market domination, both within the SFBA and beyond, adding new locations, and increasing business through delivery and catering. Dabba's humble food truck origins quickly grew to a brick-and-mortar location in 2016, adding a sizeable delivery and catering business and has a second location opening in San Francisco's Marina neighborhood this spring. Barke and Markoe are also currently looking for a second location for Media Noche in the Marina—a fast-fine dream for its high foot traffic.

Bililies is preparing to open his fourth Souvla location this spring on Chestnut Street in the Marina. When pressed to reveal his next move and how he sees the future expansion of the brand, he admits that he is now looking outside San Francisco. "Our narrative, our growth approach, really focuses on being on iconic streets, in iconic neighborhoods, in iconic cities," Bililies explains. "When you look at what we've done in San Francisco, it really lives up to that."

—

Left: Slow cooked kohlrabi, pumpernickel rye porridge, spicy mustard vinaigraitte, The Charter Oak Restaurant.

From Haute to Half Moon Bay

Words by Jessica Battilana
Photography by Daniela Velasco

In many ways, Scott Clark is the archetypical chef. He did what so many of them do: fueled by an unwavering obsession, he dropped out of college to cook, first at his hometown restaurant in Virginia, then further afield in the San Francisco Bay Area, honing his skills and rising through the kitchen ranks. Eventually, he became the chef de cuisine at Saison, a three Michelin-starred San Francisco restaurant widely considered one of the world's best. And then he did what most don't: he walked away from it all.

Standing in the converted railcar kitchen of Dad's Luncheonette, the funky roadside joint he and his partner Alexis Liu opened last year, Clark recalls a conversation he had years ago with Corey Lee, the chef-owner of another San Francisco fine-dining restaurant, Benu, where Clark worked prior to Saison.

"I was out of my depth at Benu. It was the big league. The first day, the other cooks started saying words that I just didn't understand. I was drowning in new vocabulary," he says. Having convinced himself that fine-dining kitchens were where he belonged, Clark stayed on, despite his struggles. About a year into his time at Benu, chef Lee took him aside. "He looked at me and said, 'Are you sure you want to do this? Cook this kind of food?' I assured him that I did. Then Corey looked me dead-on and said, 'I'm not sure you do.'"

As we talk, Clark leans against the counter of the luncheonette's petite kitchen, bleached tips of hair peeking out from beneath his hat, and looks out the window, as he cracks a smile. "Corey may have been right."

It took Clark a bit of time to come to the realization himself. He thought perhaps the restaurant was the problem, so he left Benu for the job at Saison, where he worked for three years, churning out elaborate tasting menus and helping the kitchen earn its third Michelin star.

It was the birth of his daughter Frost, now two, that caused Clark to reconsider his path. "I was not pulling my weight at

Chef Scott Clark.

Hamburger sandwich, Mushroom sandwich, Roasted celeriac soup, Homemade potato chips.

home, but I couldn't figure out any other way to work in that kitchen other than 16 hours a day, six days a week. I really started thinking: Do I want to cook wild rice and be an asshole for the rest of my life?" There's some irony here—as he says this, he's garnishing a steaming bowl of curried carrot soup with puffed, wild rice for a regular.

He and Liu stumbled across the luncheonette, which in its previous incarnation was a hot dog joint painted a psychedelic shade of yellow. Located in the sleepy town of Half Moon Bay, 20-or-so miles south of San Francisco and a few miles from the site of the legendary Mavericks surfing competition, the luncheonette presented Clark with an exit strategy from the fine-dining trap. This was a restaurant he could afford to run on his own terms. Those terms include a short work week (Dad's is only open Thursday through Sunday)—hours that afford him time with his kid, time surfing, and time sourcing ingredients for the restaurant. "I use a lot of the same purveyors that I used at Saison. Except, here, the carrots are $6.50 instead of $400."

Having internalized the mechanics of fine-dining, Clark pivoted sharply, bringing his skills and high-quality ingredients to a stripped down, casual venue, serving dependable, familiar food. Nothing costs more than $15. And nothing has changed since he and Liu opened the luncheonette in February of 2017.

There's a burger made with local beef that's seared on the griddle, topped with cheese, and sandwiched between two slices of aioli-smeared white bread with crisp, local lettuce and some pickled onions. There's a vegetarian version, swapping the beef patty for a cluster of maitake mushrooms, which are cooked in clarified butter on the flat-top and finished with a runny egg. A sprightly salad embellished with foraged, edible flowers and herbs, a daily soup, and freshly-fried potato chips dusted with nutritional yeast round out the menu. And there's always one sweet item, like kumquat bread pudding. It's

approachable, recognizable food, made with care and integrity, a laid-back expression of the rules of cooking and hospitality Clark learned working in high-end restaurants. Says Clark, "I've stopped worrying about whether I'm better or worse [than other chefs]. I just want to be the best father and partner I can be."

Here, on this 25-ton hunk of steel, Clark seems to have found what drives him, and it's not just Michelin stars or cooking. From the kitchen he shouts out to customers, calling them by name, telling them to drive carefully and asking how they are. "S.O.S.," replies one older gentleman named Bobby, who sits on a stool at the counter: "Same-Old Shit."

"I always knew I was going to cook," says Clark, as he smashes a beef patty on the griddle with the back of his spatula. "When I dropped out of college that's what I told my friends. I know everyone thought I was going to fail. It was like a hot iron on my ass everyday. That determination not to fail—I ate it like oatmeal for breakfast."

I ask him whether he thinks Dad's is a success. "This train car is a lifestyle project. It's helped me figure out what life is, what's important, and what's happening on this [planet]. It's my way to stay sane." I take that as a yes.

–

1
4
1

Conscientious Dietary Preferences

Words by Andréa Morrisette

Northern California, the land of sun-kissed farms, sweeping coastal views, and fog-covered cities, is also home to the Alice Waters philosophy of cooking, year-round growing seasons, and the proliferation of farmer's markets overflowing with local, organic produce.

What began as a backlash towards 1950s consumerism grew into a longing for whole foods and quality produce—farmed locally, thoughtfully, and seasonally—cooked in a manner preserving the integrity and freshness of the ingredients.

"I don't think you come to San Francisco to cook any other way," says Stuart Brioza, who, along with his wife Nicole Krasinski, is the force behind San Francisco's cult-status restaurants The Progress and State Bird Provisions. "There were comments years ago that the Bay Area does nothing with its food. That's really not the truth. We are just so attuned with having a delicate hand when needed. I couldn't imagine being in a place where people are over-manipulating food. We should always look to the ingredients and ask, 'How do we make these items that people have worked so hard to grow...just pop?'"

At Duna Kitchen [it is closed as of June 2018, with plans to reopen]—a paean to Central European peasant food—owners Nick Balla and his wife Cortney Burns have spun a shared cultural heritage into a culinary manifesto. "We both grew up eating sauerkraut and miso and other ingredients that would almost never be seen on a restaurant menu when we were younger cooks," says Balla. "The farm-to-table movement brought peasant flavors into the mainstream and helped make it possible for us to build our careers here with ingredients we love," says Balla, who recently closed the brick-and-mortar and is consulting with private clients until he and Burns open a new location.

The term "farm-to-table" has been overused, and at restaurants elsewhere in the country, has strayed from its meaning. Yet willfully admitting it or not, chefs across the San Francisco Bay Area are still actively adhering to its principal tenets. "I think it's because it's just so easy to do here—it's pretty much a no-brainer," says Sarah Rich, one half of the chef-couple team behind Rich Table, and its sister restaurant RT Rotisserie. "We have such ease of access to everything local, seasonal, organic—all of it."

"Northern California has such an incredible bounty of farms and fresh produce," says chef George Meza of his vegetable-driven menu at Onsen. "California is truly home to the world's best vegetables. Our farmers are just as passionate as our chefs when it comes to experimenting with new hybrids and heirloom varieties of produce. Farmers are responsible for encouraging chefs to cook thoughtfully with seasonality in mind."

The pursuit and appreciation of quality food is so ingrained in northern California's conscious that it is no longer a concerted "movement;" rather, it's a way of daily life. Chefs no longer struggle to source locally, and diners don't need to be educated about the benefits of organic or the merits of heirloom. The new frontier is how to hospitably navigate dietary restrictions, the self-imposed byproduct of commitment to clean and responsible eating.

Chef Dave Cruz and co-owner Eric Lilavois of Little Gem in San Francisco were inspired not only by the ingredients found in the SFBA, but also by Lilavois' own food allergies and dietary restrictions (dairy, sugar, and gluten sensitivities). Little Gem quickly cultivated a loyal following for its approach to health-consciousness, delivering flavorful dishes sans gluten, dairy, and refined sugars. "The social conscience of SFBA residents is driven by what they feel are moral imperatives," says Cruz. "Food, being important to many in our culture, plays a major role for those who feel compelled to ask questions like: 'Where is it from? How was it grown? How were the animals treated?'"

The Perennial leads San Francisco, and quite possibly the world, in its efforts toward sustainable sourcing, championing the highest levels of responsible farming practices, and considering everything down to the smallest details in the restaurant's design, service, and cuisine as a part of the big picture. "Initially, our inspiration came from becoming parents and wanting to protect our daughter's future," says Karen Leibowitz, who co-founded The Perennial with her husband and restaurant co-chef Anthony Myint. "As we dug into the concept and learned that [responsible] farming can draw down [levels of] CO2 and even reverse climate change, we felt like we found our mission in life." Quite naturally with health and ecology in mind, the menu focuses on vegetarian, vegan, and gluten-free dishes.

"We believe quality correlates to responsible practices," says Chef Jason Fox of San Francisco's progressive, one Michelin-starred Commonwealth restaurant. "Our food, in general, veers towards the healthier side, as we are very vegetable- and protein-driven, using just the right amount of fat for balance. We accommodate as many [dietary preferences] as we can. We always have dairy-, gluten-, and nut-free options for each dish. As allergies become a little more obscure, we try to work with diners to point them to appropriate dishes and possible substitutions."

Shopping seasonally at the farmer's market doesn't eliminate potential allergens from Rich Table's menu. Even still, chefs Sarah and Evan Rich make a point to honor dietary restrictions and go beyond offering gluten- or dairy-free substitutions. "We try to be thoughtful when constructing our menus," says Sarah Rich. "We really think of the whole menu and take those things in to consideration."

Rich is not alone in the sentiment that it is easier to consider the spectrum of restrictions and allergies when menu planning, and anticipate necessary changes ahead of time, rather than in the middle of service.

"We aim to accommodate allergies and restrictions with specific items designed on the menu, rather than make substitutions on dishes—that way they are well thought out," says chef Christopher Kostow of the recently

opened Charter Oak in St. Helena, and head chef of three Michelin-starred Restaurant at Meadowood. "The dishes are the best versions of what we want to do and they also accommodate people's restrictions."

The common fear is that over-accommodating guests' preferences can lead to inferior, off-recipe dishes and limit creativity in the kitchen. "We always want to make sure we are taking care of the guest, certainly when there is an allergy involved. But, we are being judged based on the quality of the food and the execution of a dish, how thoughtful it is, how good of an idea it is. It's challenging to remove little parts of a dish because it [changes the integrity of the composition]. The guest just looks at it like a thing unto itself, but it's not," says Kostow.

At the praised Lord Stanley in San Francisco, where the modern, culinary approach is equal parts American and European—evidence of their collective, international fine-dining background—chefs Rupert and Carrie Blease are also happy to oblige diners requests, but they prefer to consider a dish's integrity before making changes to their original recipe. "We don't see dietary restrictions to be a limitation; we will always try to cater to them," says Carrie Blease. "But at the same time, if the guest doesn't want or can't eat a specific dish, we would offer something different rather than changing the dish just to tend to the restrictions, as it wouldn't be as good as initially intended."

And yet some chefs are embracing the challenge to be flexible with their menu, using creative substitutions to accommodate diners' growing range of restrictions. "Limitations are often the best jumping off point for the creative process. I don't think it hinders what's happening," says Kostow.

At The Progress, Brioza has spent the last three months trying to create a vegetarian version of the kimchi recipe a friend's Korean grandmother taught him 10 years ago. Yes, there's a huge flavor difference, and he's the first to acknowledge that he's messing with the traditional to cater to

more people. "And I almost feel like that's the type of cooking we're doing," says Brioza. "We would rather have options ready for people versus having to say 'Let's make a dish for the vegan.' I'm trying to remove that. You want inclusiveness, you don't want people to feel left out. How do you do that with integrity? And that's the constant question we're after."

—

The Culinary Influence in Cocktails

Words by Lou Bustamante
Photography by Jim Sullivan

The cocktail scene for both the San Francisco Bay Area and barman Scott Baird began in restaurant bars.

Unlike New York, where the cocktail renaissance kicked off in bars like the Pegu Club and Milk & Honey, SFBA cocktails were born in restaurants. The difference in setting means mixing and drinking in the SFBA has a culinary heritage—use of culinary techniques, creative combination of ingredients bolstered by pristine bounty from local farms, and a cooperative approach to sharing information fostered by a tight community of bartenders.

Baird, for example, got his start on the kitchen side, shifting over to the bar in 2003 at César in Berkeley, a restaurant in the East Bay renowned for its spirits selection and cocktails. Across the Bay in San Francisco, other establishments were celebrating the cocktails as much as the food. Enrico's, Absinthe, and Slanted Door were restaurant bars that opened in the late 1990s and early 2000s that were seminal to the development of SFBA cocktails.

East Bay native Baird is formerly of The Bon Vivants, the bar consultant group and masterminds behind the bar Trick Dog. Best known for imaginative menus, like the one based on a Pantone color swatch book, Trick Dog features equally creative drinks, such as the GDL, a concoction that blends both tequila and mezcal with mango, lime, and pico de gallo bitters. It's an odd, yet delicious, combination that drinks like a Mexican fruit stand treat.

"You may not know that all those things go together when you see them in a cocktail on my list, but I know they do," says Baird, with a wry smile that cuts through a grey, frosted beard.

It is not accurate to classify both Baird and all SFBA bartenders as purely culinary-minded in their approach to mixing drinks. After all, it was classic Cuban mojitos that launched Enrico's bar to fame in 1992. Still, it's hard to deny the gastronomic lineage in the family tree even today.

Right: "The GDL" by Elliott Clark of Trick Dog.

The bar True Laurel, around the corner from Trick Dog, is where bar director Nicolas Torres weaves together unexpected combinations like duck fat-infused vodka, shiso, lime, and Meyer lemon in a drink called Duck Duck Goose. It's complex and rich, but surprisingly not-fatty.

"Nick [Torres] makes delicious, fun, and balanced drinks," says Baird. "The ingredients he chooses sometimes seem far out or odd on the menu, but they are integrated seamlessly."

By working closely with chef David Barzelay, Torres formulates combinations with unique ingredients, like Berto (an orange, rhubarb, and gentian bitter liqueur) or Shinko Tonic (a fermented beverage made in house using the Shinko variety of Asian pear known for its crisp sweetness) pepper the menu. Yet, as exotic as everything may read, the drinks are often simply adaptations of classics. For example, the Mai O Mai (a blend of aged rum, lime, pistachio orgeat, and curaçao, all clarified with milk, finished with a coffee-infused rum float) is an elegant remix of a Mai Tai.

Baird cautions that it takes a lot of work to make drinks with unusual combinations of ingredients taste delicious and harmonious, a lesson he learned in 2006 when he landed at Chef Loretta Keller's restaurant Coco500.

"Just because I could throw some colors on the wall and make something pretty, doesn't mean that I could paint," says Baird of his early days creating cocktails at Coco500. "[Keller] taught me technique and how to think about what I was doing."

It was at Coco500 where Keller took Baird under her wing, giving Baird books and providing a chef's perspective on incorporating ingredients and flavors. Back then, there were almost no resources, except books, chefs, and other bartenders. It was in this pre-social media era that a community of bartenders in the SFBA was forged, as a way to share information with each other, achieved by visiting each other's bars.

For Baird, the Alembic, where the late bar manager Daniel Hyatt was blending culinary techniques into his cocktails, was the bar that influenced and thrilled him the most.

"I remember he garnished a stirred-tequila drink with sliced radishes, and I was repulsed, angry, and excited," says Baird about Hyatt. "Angry and repulsed because it made sense and I hadn't thought of it. Excited, because I wanted to see what it was going to be like. It was beautiful."

While that may seem tame by today's standards, Baird says that in 2007, the first time he put a Pisco Sour cocktail on the menu with egg whites at Coco500, people were skeptical of raw egg whites in drinks. Now, he says, the cocktail IQ of guests is much higher, allowing bartenders much more freedom to expand the ingredients that can go into a cocktail.

At Loló, bar manager León Vásquez blurs the lines between kitchen and bar. Vásquez had intended to become a chef until a bartending gig altered his career path. Working closely with the kitchen and chef Jorge Martinez, Vásquez combines SFBA ingredients to create Mexican flavors. For example, the unusual-sounding "Bird and Seed" balances aquavit with chicken stock, green peas, and fennel for a slightly savory and refreshing tipple.

But it's not just the restaurant bars that are being influenced by the kitchen, it's also the neighborhood bars like the Hotsy Totsy in Albany. On the border between Berkeley and El Cerrito, it's one of Baird's favorite bars. Baird says that neighborhood bars like Hotsy Totsy have different energy and expectations, meaning that people are relaxed instead of feeling like they or others should be something else. But you can still get a great cocktail, like the Green Goddess which features a lovage syrup mixed with green chile vodka, pear liqueur, lemon, and fennel bitters, garnished with a parsley sprig.

"We don't have a kitchen at Hotsy Totsy, so the abundance of fresh herbs, fruit, and vegetables available at farmers markets is our

Left: "The Bird and the Seed" by Jorge Martinez of Lolo.
Right: "Duck Duck Goose" by Nicolas Torres of True Laurel.

"Kung Fu Pandan" by Kevin Diedrich of Pacific Cocktail Haven.

go-to for ingredients," says owner Jessica Maria. "We start with flavor combinations that work in our favorite dishes and see if we can replicate those qualities with seasonal fruits, spices and vegetables, as well as spirits and modifiers."

But invoking culinary flavors in cocktails is also allowing bartenders to re-discover their roots, like veteran barman Kevin Diedrich is doing at his bar, Pacific Cocktail Haven. Adopted as a child, Diedrich grew up not knowing much about his Filipino roots, something the barman is exploring by incorporating Filipino ingredients like pandan leaf, which has a flavor similar to buttered popcorn, into his drinks. A salted pandan leaf syrup gets mixed into his Kung Fu Pandan, which also uses Filipino rum. The herb is frequently used in rice dishes, so Diedrich mixes it with sake, along with whiskey and powdered candy cap mushrooms for a sweet-salty-savory cocktail. This drink and others show up at the monthly pop-up of Pinoy Heritage, a Filipino food project by Chef Francis Ang, further surveying those connections. Culture also influences bar manager Danny Louie at Mister Jiu's, tapping into his Chinese upbringing for his menu, which includes the Longevity, a cocktail that blends mezcal and verjus with osmanthus and scallion.

Even with all this creativity, there are some fundamentals of the bar that are universal. Baird says that to be a successful bar, you need to have a point of view and make things that taste delicious while understanding your pour costs. But you also need to be ready for anything— even a night like the first Saturday night he helped re-launch the North Beach bar 15 Romolo in 2008.

"The floor drain in the corner got blocked up. I stuck a spoon in there and [the drain pipe] was paper thin. The spoon punched a hole right through," recalled Baird. "Then, two strippers, who were still mostly nude, came charging in from the strip club below, screaming at me. I had flooded their dressing room."

It's hard to predict if the culinary roots in the SFBA will continue to bear fruit at the bar, or if the lightning-quick exchange of ideas within the industry will continue to ebb away regional differences in drinking culture. But just like North Beach will always have strip clubs, SFBA bars will continue to define and evolve cocktails in restaurants and beyond. When surrounded by local farms growing such incredible produce, and restaurants using it in interesting ways, local bartenders will find constant inspiration to shake things up.

—

1
4
9

Chinatown Revisited

Words by Sharon Brenner
Photography by Adam Goldberg

San Francisco's Chinatown is arguably one of the most historic Chinatowns in America. Centrally located and sandwiched between the Financial District and old-money Nob Hill, Chinatown is a study in contrast: It is a place rich with culture, tourist shops (some of which appear to be fronts for something else), and where locals regularly find grandparents crowding onto buses, loaded with bags brimming with delicacies from the bustling markets. It is a relatively less-affluent area of the city and an immigrant-strong community, just steps from the iconic Transamerica Building.

One could argue that opening a restaurant in this neighborhood would not be a prudent business decision, as it has been less impacted relative to other now-trendy neighborhoods impacted by San Francisco's newest wave of gentrification. But as Brandon Jew, Head Chef of the award-winning restaurant Mister Jiu's explains, for well over 100 years San Francisco's Chinatown has in fact been *the* epicenter of where contemporary Chinese and Chinese-American cuisine was showcased to the wider American dining community.

"Some of the history of San Francisco's Chinatown has been about trying to get the city as a whole to eat Chinese food, and to come to the neighborhood to understand and celebrate it," says Jew. "When we opened Mister Jiu's, I wanted to represent contemporary San Francisco dining, and specifically Chinese food in Chinatown, where, historically, contemporary Chinese and Chinese-American cuisine in America was born."

Jew, therefore, felt a strong responsibility to locate the restaurant in Chinatown, a community that has continued to maintain its cultural identity during another phase of rapid change in San Francisco that can be seen in neighborhoods like the Mission, along Divisadero Street in NoPa (North of the Panhandle), and the Dogpatch, for example. When some of the classic, long-standing restaurants in the neighborhood shuttered their doors, Jew sensed a need for someone to carry the torch to expand Chinese-American cuisine from *within*

Chinatown. As a native San Franciscan of Chinese descent, Jew felt he was a particularly compelling candidate to take on that role. "I felt like it was more important to have a restaurant in Chinatown and fail, than to be in The Mission and succeed."

Jew's urges recall his own journey in the food industry and issues of personal identity. "I struggled for a time with why I was cooking," he admits. "Being in Chinatown has helped me find my purpose. It's an inspirational space that has given me more than I ever expected." Whether consciously or not, he is serving by example for future generations of Chinese-American chefs, and helping to shape the evolution of the neighborhood.

Under his vision, Mister Jiu's stands out as a unique dining destination in the city. Located down a narrow alley illuminated by neon signs, diners enter a potentially unfamiliar world to experience the Chinatown of today and yesterday, regardless of whether they are Chinese, Chinese-American, or neither, regardless of their cultural background.

"I want the menu to have recognizable, nostalgic elements, and for some people that refers to sweet and sour pork, which is great, because it's delicious. But there are more nutritious and interesting ways of evoking nostalgia, too. Likewise, we want our Chinese clientele to appreciate our innovation, while still being able to recognize the food as Chinese." Anchored in traditional techniques and flavors of Chinese cookery, Jew's menu brings a diverse selection of high-quality, local products that makes Mister Jiu's a distinctly Chinese-San Franciscan vanguard of the Chinatown of today.

Like its predecessors, Mister Jiu's entices people to Chinatown, drawing renewed attention to the neighborhood with Jew writing a new chapter in the canon of Chinese-American cuisine. His passion therefore represents something novel for the Chinatown of today; an open invitation to diners to immerse themselves in something surprising yet nostalgic, to simultaneously engage with a world that can be both familiar and totally new.

—

Whole Dungeness Crab, sticky rice, peanut, coconut and cured duck yolk. Crab tomalley and duck egg custard.

Chef Brandon Jew.

Chilled beef tendon with blood orange and Lanzhou chili crisp.

addresses and coordinates

00
20th Century Café
198 Gough St, San Francisco, CA 94102
37.77493° N, 122.42239° W

A
AL's Place
1499 Valencia St, San Francisco, CA 94110
37.74905° N, 122.42013° W

Arsicault Bakery
397 Arguello Blvd, San Francisco, CA 94118
37.78342° N, 122.45930° W

Ashes & Diamonds Winery
4130 Howard Ln, Napa, CA 94558
38.344250° N, 122.32628° W

Atelier Crenn
3127 Fillmore St, San Francisco, CA 94123
37.79834° N, 122.43594° W

B
B. Patisserie
2821 California St, San Francisco, CA 94115
37.78787° N, 122.44086° W

Bakesale Betty
5098 Telegraph Ave, Oakland, CA 94609
37.83705° N, 122.26206° W

Banh Cuon Tay Ho
2895 Senter Rd # 110, San Jose, CA 95111
37.29785° N, 121.83828° W

Barzotto
1270 Valencia St, San Francisco, CA 94110
37.75252° N, 122.42091° W

Beer Shed
95 Linden St, Oakland, CA 94607
37.79949° N, 122.28790° W

Benkyodo Co
1747 Buchanan St,
San Francisco, CA 94115, USA
37.78636° N, 122.43010° W

Benu
22 Hawthorne St, San Francisco, CA 94105
37.78545° N, 122.39903° W

Black Jet Baking Co
833 Cortland Ave, San Francisco, CA 94110
37.73910° N, 122.41414° W

Blue Hill at Stone Barns
630 Bedford Rd, Tarrytown, NY 10591
41.10401° N, 73.82895° W

C
Cala
149 Fell St, San Francisco, CA 94102
37.77607° N, 122.42040° W

Camino
3917 Grand Ave, Oakland, CA 94610
37.81840° N, 122.24520° W

Chez Panisse
1517 Shattuck Ave, Berkeley, CA 94709
37.87959° N, 122.26893° W

Coco500
500 Brannan St, San Francisco, CA 94107
37.77829° N, 122.39688° W

Commonwealth
2224 Mission St, San Francisco, CA 94110
37.76132° N, 122.41964° W

Continuum Winery
1677 Sage Canyon Rd, St Helena, CA 94574
38.48338° N, 122.35496° W

Cotogna
490 Pacific Ave, San Francisco, CA 94133
37.79744° N, 122.40357° W

Cowgirl Creamery
One Embarcadero #17, San Francisco, CA 94105
37.79580° N, 122.39348 ° W

Craftsman & Wolves
746 Valencia St, San Francisco, CA 94110
37.76091° N, 122.42171° W

D
Dabba
71 Stevenson St, San Francisco, CA 94105
37.78927° N, 122.39958° W

Dad's Luncheonette
225 Cabrillo Hwy S, Half Moon Bay, CA 94019
37.46490° N, 122.43318° W

Dandelion Chocolate
740 Valencia St,
San Francisco, CA 94110, USA
37.76103° N, 122.42172° W

Darioush Winery
4240 Silverado Trail, Napa, CA 94558
38.36751° N, 122.29456° W

Deli Board
1058 Folsom St, San Francisco, CA 94103
37.77771° N, 122.40714° W

Dynamo Donut & Coffee
2760 24th St, San Francisco, CA 94110
37.75307° N, 122.41806° W

E
Eleven Madison Park
11 Madison Ave, New York, NY 10010
40.74151° N, 73.98696° W

El Molino Central
11 Central Ave, Sonoma, CA 95476
38.31510° N, 122.48199° W

Enrico's
504 Broadway, San Francisco, CA 94133
37.79812° N, 122.40564° W

F
Frances
3870 17th St, San Francisco, CA 94114
37.76276° N, 122.43222° W

Fournée Bakery
2912 Domingo Ave, Berkeley, CA 94705
37.85877° N, 122.24422° W

Fugetsu-do
315 E 1st St, Los Angeles, CA 90012
34.05020° N, 118.24032° W

G
Glen Ellen Star
13648 Arnold Dr, Glen Ellen, CA 95442
38.36430° N, 122.52461° W

Golden Gate Fortune Cookie Factory
178 Townsend St, San Francisco, CA 94107
37.79570° N, 122.40734° W

H
Hodo Soy
2923 Adeline St, Oakland, CA 94608
37.82157° N, 122.28215° W

Hog Island Oyster Co.
20215 Shoreline Hwy, Marshall, CA 94940
38.16212° N, 122.89354° W

Hong Kong Noodle Company
710 E 9th Pl, Los Angeles, CA 90021
34.03629° N, 118.25094° W

Hotsy Totsy
601 San Pablo Ave, Albany, CA 94706
37.89504° N, 122.30018° W

Ijji Sushi
252 Divisadero St, San Francisco, CA 94117
37.771441° N, 122.43695° W

J
Jardinière
300 Grove St, San Francisco, CA 94102
37.77816° N, 122.42179° W

K
Kin Khao Thai Eatery
55 Cyril Magnin St, San Francisco, CA 94102
37.78519° N, 122.40936° W

Kusakabe
584 Washington St, San Francisco, CA 94111
37.79569° N, 122.40290° W

L
La Palma Mexicatessen
2884 24th St, San Francisco, CA 94110
37.75298° N, 122.40996° W

Liguria Bakery
1700 Stockton St, San Francisco, CA 94133
37.80152° N, 122.40927° W

Littorai Wines
788 Gold Ridge Rd, Sebastopol, CA 95472
38.38491° N, 122.86510° W

Liho Liho Yacht Club
871 Sutter St, San Francisco, CA 94109
37.78823° N, 122.41459° W

Little Gem
400 Grove St, C1, San Francisco, CA 94102
37.77787° N, 122.42347° W

Loló
974 Valencia St, San Francisco, CA 94110
37.75732° N, 122.42141° W

Lord Stanley
2065 Polk St, San Francisco, CA 94109
37.79576° N, 122.42202° W

M
M.H Bread + Butter
101 San Anselmo Ave, San Anselmo, CA, 94960
37.97063° N, 122.56155° W

Manresa
320 Village Ln, Los Gatos, CA 95030
37.22739° N, 121.98076° W

Manresa Bread
276 N Santa Cruz Ave, Los Gatos, CA 95030
37.22705° N, 121.98100° W

Marla Bakery
276 N Santa Cruz Ave, Los Gatos, CA 95030
37.77551° N, 122.49771° W

Media Noche
3465 19th St, San Francisco, CA 94110
37.75998° N, 122.42073° W

Mister Jiu's
28 Waverly Pl, San Francisco, CA 94108
37.79372° N, 122.40665° W

Mr. Holmes Bakehouse
1042 Larkin St, San Francisco, CA 94109
37.78763° N, 122.28215° W

N
Neighbor Bakehouse
2343 3rd St #100, San Francisco, CA 94107
37.75962° N,122.38817° W

O
Octavia
1701 Octavia St, San Francisco, CA 94109
37.78797° N, 122.42713° W

Onsen Bath and Restaurant
466 Eddy St, San Francisco, CA 94109
37.78386° N, 122.41539° W

Outerlands
4001 Judah St, San Francisco, CA 94122
37.76026° N, 122.50502° W

P
Pacific Cocktail Haven
4001 Judah St, San Francisco, CA 94122
37.76026° N, 122.50502° W

Padrecito
4001 Judah St, San Francisco, CA 94122
37.76026° N, 122.50502° W

Pegu Club
4001 Judah St, San Francisco, CA 94122
37.76026° N, 122.50502° W

Petit Crenn
609 Hayes St, San Francisco, CA 94102
37.77635° N, 122.42652° W

Pho Ga Nha
930 Story Rd, San Jose, CA 95122
37.33050° N, 121.85626° W

Pho Tick Tock
137 E 3rd Ave, San Mateo, CA 94401
37.56464° N, 122.32402° W

Piccino
1001 Minnesota St, San Francisco, CA 94107
37.75753° N, 122.38995° W
Posie
4001 Judah St, San Francisco, CA 94122
37.76026° N, 122.50502° W

Protéa
6488 Washington St., Yountville, CA 94599
38.39990° N, 122.35908° W

Q
Quince
470 Pacific Ave, San Francisco, CA 94133
37.79744° N, 122.40357° W

R
Ramey Wine Cellars
25 Healdsburg Ave, Healdsburg, CA 95448
38.60357° N, 122.86256° W

Reem's California
3301 E 12th St #133, Oakland, CA 94601
37.77584° N, 122.22479° W

Rich Table
199 Gough St, San Francisco, CA 94102
37.77487° N, 122.42281° W

Ridge Vineyards
17100 Montebello Rd, Cupertino, CA 95014
37.29961° N, 122.11583° W

Ridge Vineyards Lytton Springs
650 Lytton Springs Rd, Healdsburg, CA 95448
38.65912° N, 122.88565° W

Rintaro
82 14th St, San Francisco, CA 94103
37.76881° N, 122.41511° W

S
Sababa
3204, 329 Kearny St, San Francisco, CA 94108
37.79117° N, 122.40435° W

Saison
178 Townsend St, San Francisco, CA 94107
37.77953° N, 122.39226° W

Scribe Winery
2100 Denmark St, Sonoma, CA 95476
38.27607° N, 122.41451° W

Single Thread
131 North St, Healdsburg, CA 95448
38.61213° N, 122.86984° W

Souvla
517 Hayes St, San Francisco, CA 94102
37.77645° N, 122.42500° W

State Bird Provisions
1529 Fillmore St, San Francisco, CA 94115
37.78370° N, 122.43299° W

T
Tacolicius
741 Valencia St, San Francisco, CA 94110
37.76096° N, 122.42134° W

Tartine Bakery
600 Guerrero St, San Francisco, CA 94110
37.76141° N,122.42409° W

Tartine Manufactory
595 Alabama St, San Francisco, CA 94110
37.76184° N,122.41194° W

The Charter Oak Restaurant
1050 Charter Oak Ave, St Helena, CA 94574
38.50176° N, 122.46402° W

The French Laundry
6640 Washington St, Yountville, CA 94599
38.40442° N, 122.36497° W

The Mill
736 Divisadero St, San Francisco, CA 94117
37.77646° N, 122.43783° W

The Kebabery
4201 Market St, Oakland, CA 94608
37.83254° N, 122.27369° W

The Perennial
59 9th St, San Francisco, CA 94103
37.77677° N, 122.41521° W

The Progress
1525 Fillmore St, San Francisco, CA 94115
37.78368° N, 122.43299° W

The Restaurant at Meadowood
900 Meadowood Ln, St Helena, CA 94574
38.52255° N, 122.46747° W

Three Babes Bakeshop
2501 Phelps St, San Francisco, CA 94124
37.72970° N, 122.40028° W

Trick Dog
3010 20th St, San Francisco, CA 94110
37.75922° N, 122.41121° W

Tropisueño
75 Yerba Buena Ln, San Francisco, CA 94103
37.78535° N, 122.40386° W

True Laurel
753 Alabama St, San Francisco, CA 94110
37.75951° N, 122.41144° W

W
Willow's Inn on Lummi Island
2579 W Shore Dr, Lummi Island, WA 98262
48.73553° N, 122.71904° W

Wise Sons Jewish Delicatessen
3150 24th St, San Francisco, CA 94110
37.75253° N, 122.41533° W

Wonton Food Inc.
220 222 Moore St, Brooklyn, NY 11206
37.75253° N, 73.9355° W